P9-DDC-580

JULIUS CAESAR

EDITOR-IN-CHIEF: Nancy Toff
EXECUTIVE EDITOR: Remmel T. Nunn
MANAGING EDITOR: Karyn Gullen Browne
COPY CHIEF: Perry Scott King
ART DIRECTOR: Giannella Garrett

Staff for JULIUS CAESAR:

SENIOR EDITOR: John W. Selfridge
ASSISTANT EDITORS: Maria Behan, Pierre Hauser, Kathleen McDermott, Bert Yaeger
COPY EDITORS: Gillian Bucky, Sean Dolan
DESIGN ASSISTANT: Jill Goldreyer
PICTURE RESEARCH: Susan B. Hamburger
LAYOUT: Debbie Jay
PRODUCTION COORDINATOR: Alma Rodriguez
COVER ILLUSTRATION: Richard Leonard

CREATIVE DIRECTOR: Harold Steinberg

Printed and bound in the United States of America.

Frontispiece courtesy of Giraudon/Art Resource

First Printing

Library of Congress Cataloging in Publication Data

Bruns, Roger. JULIUS CAESAR

(World leaders past & present)
Bibliography: p.
Includes index.
1. Caesar, Julius—Juvenile literature. 2. Rome—History—Republic, 265–30 B.C.—Juvenile literature. 3. Heads of state—Rome—Biography—Juvenile literature. 4. Generals—Rome—Biography—Juvenile literature. [1. Caesar, Julius. 2. Heads of state. 3. Generals. 4. Rome—History—Republic, 265–30 B.C.] I. Title. II. Series: World leaders past & present.
DG261.B78 1987 973'.05'0924 [B] [92] 87-6339

ISBN 0-87754-514-6

Contents

WORLD LEADERS PAST & PRESENT

JULIUS CAESAR

Roger Bruns

CHELSEA HOUSE PUBLISHERS
NEW YORK
NEW HAVEN PHILADELPHIA

CHELSEA HOUSE PUBLISHERS

WORLD LEADERS PAST & PRESENT

ADENAUER
ALEXANDER THE GREAT
MARC ANTONY
KING ARTHUR
ATATÜRK
ATTLEE
BEGIN
BEN-GURION
BISMARCK
LÉON BLUM
BOLÍVAR
CESARE BORGIA
BRANDT
BREZHNEV
CAESAR
CALVIN
CASTRO
CATHERINE THE GREAT
CHARLEMAGNE
CHIANG KAI-SHEK
CHURCHILL
CLEMENCEAU
CLEOPATRA
CORTÉS
CROMWELL
DANTON
DE GAULLE
DE VALERA
DISRAELI
EISENHOWER
ELEANOR OF AQUITAINE
QUEEN ELIZABETH I
FERDINAND AND ISABELLA
FRANCO
FREDERICK THE GREAT
INDIRA GANDHI
MOHANDAS GANDHI
GARIBALDI
GENGHIS KHAN
GLADSTONE
GORBACHEV
HAMMARSKJÖLD
HENRY VIII
HENRY OF NAVARRE
HINDENBURG
HITLER
HO CHI MINH
HUSSEIN
IVAN THE TERRIBLE
ANDREW JACKSON
JEFFERSON
JOAN OF ARC
POPE JOHN XXIII
LYNDON JOHNSON
JUÁREZ
JOHN F. KENNEDY
KENYATTA
KHOMEINI
KHRUSHCHEV
MARTIN LUTHER KING, JR.
KISSINGER
LENIN
LINCOLN
LLOYD GEORGE
LOUIS XIV
LUTHER
JUDAS MACCABEUS
MAO ZEDONG
MARY, QUEEN OF SCOTS
GOLDA MEIR
METTERNICH
MUSSOLINI
NAPOLEON
NASSER
NEHRU
NERO
NICHOLAS II
NIXON
NKRUMAH
PERICLES
PERÓN
QADDAFI
ROBESPIERRE
ELEANOR ROOSEVELT
FRANKLIN D. ROOSEVELT
THEODORE ROOSEVELT
SADAT
STALIN
SUN YAT-SEN
TAMERLANE
THATCHER
TITO
TROTSKY
TRUDEAU
TRUMAN
VICTORIA
WASHINGTON
WEIZMANN
WOODROW WILSON
XERXES
ZHOU ENLAI

ON LEADERSHIP

Arthur M. Schlesinger, jr.

LEADERSHIP, it may be said, is really what makes the world go round. Love no doubt smooths the passage; but love is a private transaction between consenting adults. Leadership is a public transaction with history. The idea of leadership affirms the capacity of individuals to move, inspire, and mobilize masses of people so that they act together in pursuit of an end. Sometimes leadership serves good purposes, sometimes bad; but whether the end is benign or evil, great leaders are those men and women who leave their personal stamp on history.

Now, the very concept of leadership implies the proposition that individuals can make a difference. This proposition has never been universally accepted. From classical times to the present day, eminent thinkers have regarded individuals as no more than the agents and pawns of larger forces, whether the gods and goddesses of the ancient world or, in the modern era, race, class, nation, the dialectic, the will of the people, the spirit of the times, history itself. Against such forces, the individual dwindles into insignificance.

So contends the thesis of historical determinism. Tolstoy's great novel *War and Peace* offers a famous statement of the case. Why, Tolstoy asked, did millions of men in the Napoleonic wars, denying their human feelings and their common sense, move back and forth across Europe slaughtering their fellows? "The war," Tolstoy answered, "was bound to happen simply because it was bound to happen." All prior history predetermined it. As for leaders, they, Tolstoy said, "are but the labels that serve to give a name to an end and, like labels, they have the least possible connection with the event." The greater the leader, "the more conspicuous the inevitability and the predestination of every act he commits." The leader, said Tolstoy, is "the slave of history."

Determinism takes many forms. Marxism is the determinism of class. Nazism the determinism of race. But the idea of men and women as the slaves of history runs athwart the deepest human instincts. Rigid determinism abolishes the idea of human freedom—

the assumption of free choice that underlies every move we make, every word we speak, every thought we think. It abolishes the idea of human responsibility, since it is manifestly unfair to reward or punish people for actions that are by definition beyond their control. No one can live consistently by any deterministic creed. The Marxist states prove this themselves by their extreme susceptibility to the cult of leadership.

More than that, history refutes the idea that individuals make no difference. In December 1931 a British politician crossing Park Avenue in New York City between 76th and 77th Streets around 10:30 P.M. looked in the wrong direction and was knocked down by an automobile—a moment, he later recalled, of a man aghast, a world aglare: "I do not understand why I was not broken like an eggshell or squashed like a gooseberry." Fourteen months later an American politician, sitting in an open car in Miami, Florida, was fired on by an assassin; the man beside him was hit. Those who believe that individuals make no difference to history might well ponder whether the next two decades would have been the same had Mario Constasino's car killed Winston Churchill in 1931 and Giuseppe Zangara's bullet killed Franklin Roosevelt in 1933. Suppose, in addition, that Adolf Hitler had been killed in the street fighting during the Munich *Putsch* of 1923 and that Lenin had died of typhus during World War I. What would the 20th century be like now?

For better or for worse, individuals do make a difference. "The notion that a people can run itself and its affairs anonymously," wrote the philosopher William James, "is now well known to be the silliest of absurdities. Mankind does nothing save through initiatives on the part of inventors, great or small, and imitation by the rest of us—these are the sole factors in human progress. Individuals of genius show the way, and set the patterns, which common people then adopt and follow."

Leadership, James suggests, means leadership in thought as well as in action. In the long run, leaders in thought may well make the greater difference to the world. But, as Woodrow Wilson once said, "Those only are leaders of men, in the general eye, who lead in action. . . . It is at their hands that new thought gets its translation into the crude language of deeds." Leaders in thought often invent in solitude and obscurity, leaving to later generations the tasks of imitation. Leaders in action—the leaders portrayed in this series—have to be effective in their own time.

And they cannot be effective by themselves. They must act in response to the rhythms of their age. Their genius must be adapted, in a phrase of William James's, "to the receptivities of the moment." Leaders are useless without followers. "There goes the mob," said the French politician hearing a clamor in the streets. "I am their leader. I must follow them." Great leaders turn the inchoate emotions of the mob to purposes of their own. They seize on the opportunities of their time, the hopes, fears, frustrations, crises, potentialities. They succeed when events have prepared the way for them, when the community is awaiting to be aroused, when they can provide the clarifying and organizing ideas. Leadership ignites the circuit between the individual and the mass and thereby alters history.

It may alter history for better or for worse. Leaders have been responsible for the most extravagant follies and most monstrous crimes that have beset suffering humanity. They have also been vital in such gains as humanity has made in individual freedom, religious and racial tolerance, social justice and respect for human rights.

There is no sure way to tell in advance who is going to lead for good and who for evil. But a glance at the gallery of men and women in *World Leaders—Past and Present* suggests some useful tests.

One test is this: do leaders lead by force or by persuasion? By command or by consent? Through most of history leadership was exercised by the divine right of authority. The duty of followers was to defer and to obey. "Theirs not to reason why,/ Theirs but to do and die." On occasion, as with the so-called "enlightened despots" of the 18th century in Europe, absolutist leadership was animated by humane purposes. More often, absolutism nourished the passion for domination, land, gold and conquest and resulted in tyranny.

The great revolution of modern times has been the revolution of equality. The idea that all people should be equal in their legal condition has undermined the old structure of authority, hierarchy and deference. The revolution of equality has had two contrary effects on the nature of leadership. For equality, as Alexis de Tocqueville pointed out in his great study *Democracy in America*, might mean equality in servitude as well as equality in freedom.

"I know of only two methods of establishing equality in the political world," Tocqueville wrote. "Rights must be given to every citizen, or none at all to anyone . . . save one, who is the master of all." There was no middle ground "between the sovereignty of all and the absolute power of one man." In his astonishing prediction of 20th-century totalitarian dictatorship, Tocqueville explained how the revolution of equality could lead to the *"Führerprinzip"* and more terrible absolutism than the world had ever known.

But when rights are given to every citizen and the sovereignty of all is established, the problem of leadership takes a new form, becomes more exacting than ever before. It is easy to issue commands and enforce them by the rope and the stake, the concentration camp and the *gulag*. It is much harder to use argument and achievement to overcome opposition and win consent. The Founding Fathers of the United States understood the difficulty. They believed that history had given them the opportunity to decide, as Alexander Hamilton wrote in the first Federalist Paper, whether men are indeed capable of basing government on "reflection and choice, or whether they are forever destined to depend . . . on accident and force."

Government by reflection and choice called for a new style of leadership and a new quality of followership. It required leaders to be responsive to popular concerns, and it required followers to be active and informed participants in the process. Democracy does not eliminate emotion from politics; sometimes it fosters demagoguery; but it is confident that, as the greatest of democratic leaders put it, you cannot fool all of the people all of the time. It measures leadership by results and retires those who overreach or falter or fail.

It is true that in the long run despots are measured by results too. But they can postpone the day of judgment, sometimes indefinitely, and in the meantime they can do infinite harm. It is also true that democracy is no guarantee of virtue and intelligence in government, for the voice of the people is not necessarily the voice of God. But democracy, by assuring the right of opposition, offers built-in resistance to the evils inherent in absolutism. As the theologian Reinhold Niebuhr summed it up, "Man's capacity for justice makes democracy possible, but man's inclination to injustice makes democracy necessary."

A second test for leadership is the end for which power is sought. When leaders have as their goal the supremacy of a master race or the promotion of totalitarian revolution or the acquisition and exploitation of colonies or the protection of greed and privilege or the preservation of personal power, it is likely that their leadership will do little to advance the cause of humanity. When their goal is the abolition of slavery, the liberation of women, the enlargement of opportunity for the poor and powerless, the extension of equal rights to racial minorities, the defense of the freedoms of expression and opposition, it is likely that their leadership will increase the sum of human liberty and welfare.

Leaders have done great harm to the world. They have also conferred great benefits. You will find both sorts in this series. Even "good" leaders must be regarded with a certain wariness. Leaders are not demigods; they put on their trousers one leg after another just like ordinary mortals. No leader is infallible, and every leader needs to be reminded of this at regular intervals. Irreverence irritates leaders but is their salvation. Unquestioning submission corrupts leaders and demands followers. Making a cult of a leader is always a mistake. Fortunately hero worship generates its own antidote. "Every hero," said Emerson, "becomes a bore at last."

The signal benefit the great leaders confer is to embolden the rest of us to live according to our own best selves, to be active, insistent, and resolute in affirming our own sense of things. For great leaders attest to the reality of human freedom against the supposed inevitabilities of history. And they attest to the wisdom and power that may lie within the most unlikely of us, which is why Abraham Lincoln remains the supreme example of great leadership. A great leader, said Emerson, exhibits new possibilities to all humanity. "We feed on genius. . . . Great men exist that there may be greater men."

Great leaders, in short, justify themselves by emancipating and empowering their followers. So humanity struggles to master its destiny, remembering with Alexis de Tocqueville: "It is true that around every man a fatal circle is traced beyond which he cannot pass; but within the wide verge of that circle he is powerful and free; as it is with man, so with communities."

1
The Ides of March

> ***We petty men walk under his [Caesar's] huge legs, and peep about to find ourselves dishonorable graves.***
> —GAIUS CASSIUS LONGINUS
> Roman politician,
> in Shakespeare's
> *Julius Caesar*

Through the narrow streets of Rome, Julius Caesar was borne toward the Forum, the center of Roman public life, on a litter carried by his servants. A throng of people followed in his path, cheering exuberantly. Caesar had spent many years struggling to increase his political power, at every turn meeting resistance from an entrenched group of conservative senators who sought to preserve the Roman republic — an unofficial oligarchy of those with the most money and the fewest scruples. He was now revered by the multitude as a symbol of authority and might, a man legendary and heroic. After securing key government positions, large sums of money, and growing influence, Caesar had finally established himself as dictator of Rome. Whenever he appeared in public, people gathered to pay him homage. Some worshiped him as a god. His face appeared on Roman coins, an honor never before accorded to a living man. All over Rome, statues of the ruler had been erected.

But on this day, March 15, 44 B.C., called by Romans the "Ides of March," mixed in with the cheers and adulation were omens foretelling imminent doom. A soothsayer had mysteriously told Caesar to beware of sinister forces. His wife, Calpurnia, had dreamt that he was viciously murdered and had

In 45 B.C. Roman statesman Julius Caesar (left) was named dictator for life, having overthrown the senatorial oligarchy that dominated Roman politics. On March 15, 44 B.C. (the Ides of March), his wife Calpurnia dreamed of his impending assassination and begged him to stay home.

THE BETTMANN ARCHIVE

THE BETTMANN ARCHIVE

Julius Caesar is stabbed to death by a group of conspirators in full view of the assembled Roman Senate. One of the leaders of the group was Marcus Brutus, whom the Roman dictator had considered an ally.

begged him not to leave the house. Although clearly upset by these omens, Caesar had decided to go to the Senate house anyway. Having climbed to the pinnacle of power on his own strength of will, on his courage, his guile, his ambition and pride, he would not be intimidated by mere dreams and portents.

As Caesar reached the Senate, a crowd of people surrounded him, some handing him petitions and notes, others kissing his hand. Roman historians would later claim that one of the notes was a warning to Caesar of an assassination plot. In the excitement of the moment, Caesar did not bother to read the messages. Instead, he entered the building.

The members of the Senate rose as the ruler entered the hall and took his place of honor. Soon a group of men gathered around Caesar as if to engage him in conversation. One man, Tillius Cimber, knelt before Caesar seeking his support on a political matter. As Caesar walked by, Cimber grabbed the dictator's purple robe and violently pulled it down from his shoulder. This was the signal.

Suddenly, several men pulled long daggers from their tunics. A man named Casca struck a blow at Caesar from behind, piercing his shoulder. When the ruler, startled and horrified, turned around to challenge his attacker, he faced a sea of upraised daggers. He was quickly engulfed. In the frenzied assault, the assassins plunged their weapons repeatedly into the flesh of the disbelieving ruler. Cae-

If there be any in this assembly, any dear friend of Caesar's, to him I say that Brutus's love to Caesar was no less than his. If, then, that friend demand why Brutus rose against Caesar, this is my answer — not that I loved Caesar less, but that I loved Rome more.

—MARCUS BRUTUS
Roman politician,
addressing the Senate after
Caesar's murder,
in Shakespeare's
Julius Caesar

sar flailed feebly at the attackers with his only weapon, a fountain pen, and finally slumped to the ground and covered his head with his toga. Blood spilled from his mangled body, drenching the floor, but he still had the energy to utter a short, haunting cry. It was addressed to one of the conspirators whom he had thought was his ally and friend, Marcus Brutus. As the bloody daggers finished their work, Caesar said weakly, "*Et tu, Brute!*" (And you, too, Brutus!) Then he was dead.

Two millenia later, the assassination of Julius Caesar remains a compelling and dramatic moment in history. Scholars, statesmen, and philosophers continue to ask whether the assassination was an unjustified act of political terror, motivated by self-interest and spite, or an altruistic attempt to preserve the remnants of Roman democracy by eliminating a tyrant.

The story of Caesar is a story of power — its achievement, its exercise and abuses, its loss. As we try to understand the circumstances of Caesar's rise to power and his fall, we must look back nearly 2,000 years. It is difficult to imagine a time so far removed from our present era, a time of charioteers and gladiators, of marble temples honoring a pantheon of gods, of people dressed in togas, of documents written on parchment.

Our knowledge of Julius Caesar and Roman history comes from several sources. Archaeological examination of the crumbling remains of Roman buildings tells us part of the story; statues, coins, paintings, armor, and weapons provide further clues. Other information is provided by the surviving histories, epic poems, and plays of the period.

The Greek historian Plutarch and the Roman historian Suetonius offer us a glimpse into Caesar's world, but the most influential writer on Caesar remains the British playwright William Shakespeare. It is in his play *Julius Caesar*, written more than 16 centuries after Caesar's death, that the characters of Caesar, Brutus, and Calpurnia truly come alive. Although Shakespeare had read the works of Plutarch, the Elizabethan playwright took many lib-

THE BETTMANN ARCHIVE

Plutarch, a Greek historian of the first century A.D. His most important work, *Parallel Lives*, matched biographies of noted Greeks with biographies of their Roman counterparts. Plutarch paired Caesar with Alexander the Great, the Greek general who conquered most of the known world before his 30th birthday.

THE BETTMANN ARCHIVE

William Shakespeare, the 16th- and 17th-century British playwright, brought Roman history vividly to life in the drama *Julius Caesar*. Despite some inaccuracies the play remains an important source for biographers of Caesar.

erties with the Greek writer's history, partially basing his characters on well-known Renaissance figures and endowing them with attitudes resembling those of his own era. Still, his play remains a major source for biographers of Caesar.

In some of the interpretations of Caesar's life, we read of his lust for power. Vain, drunk with ambition, he relished the worship of the crowds, craved adulation, thirsted for greater and greater glory. In other accounts Caesar is portrayed as a fair, even gentle statesman, generous to the masses, granting clemency to the conquered — a farsighted patriot with visions of a magnificent empire for his country and a just society for its people.

Both of these interpretations, although wildly at odds, contain part of the truth. Like most historical figures, Julius Caesar was a complex individual with a multitude of often conflicting traits.

When Caesar was born, sometime around 100 B.C., Rome was a flourishing civilization, boasting a glorious history, a rich culture, and an advanced — if corrupt — form of government. According to legend, the city had been founded in 753 B.C. when the twins Romulus and Remus united into a single political entity the herdsmen and farmers who inhabited the area's many hills. In its early years, the city was ruled by a series of kings. After the last king, Tarquin the Proud, was expelled in 509 B.C., a republic with semi-democratic institutions was established. Primary authority was vested in two consuls, who were elected to one-year terms; they were supplemented by many levels of administrators and by the Senate, which was intended to play only an advisory role.

At first the rigid social hierarchy that had developed during the regal period remained intact, as lesser families, known as *plebians*, remained bound by the institution of clientship to the more powerful ones, called *patricians*, who controlled all political offices, including the citizens' assembly, the *comitia centuria*. Over the next two centuries, the Roman political system became increasingly democratic. Eventually, the plebians were granted

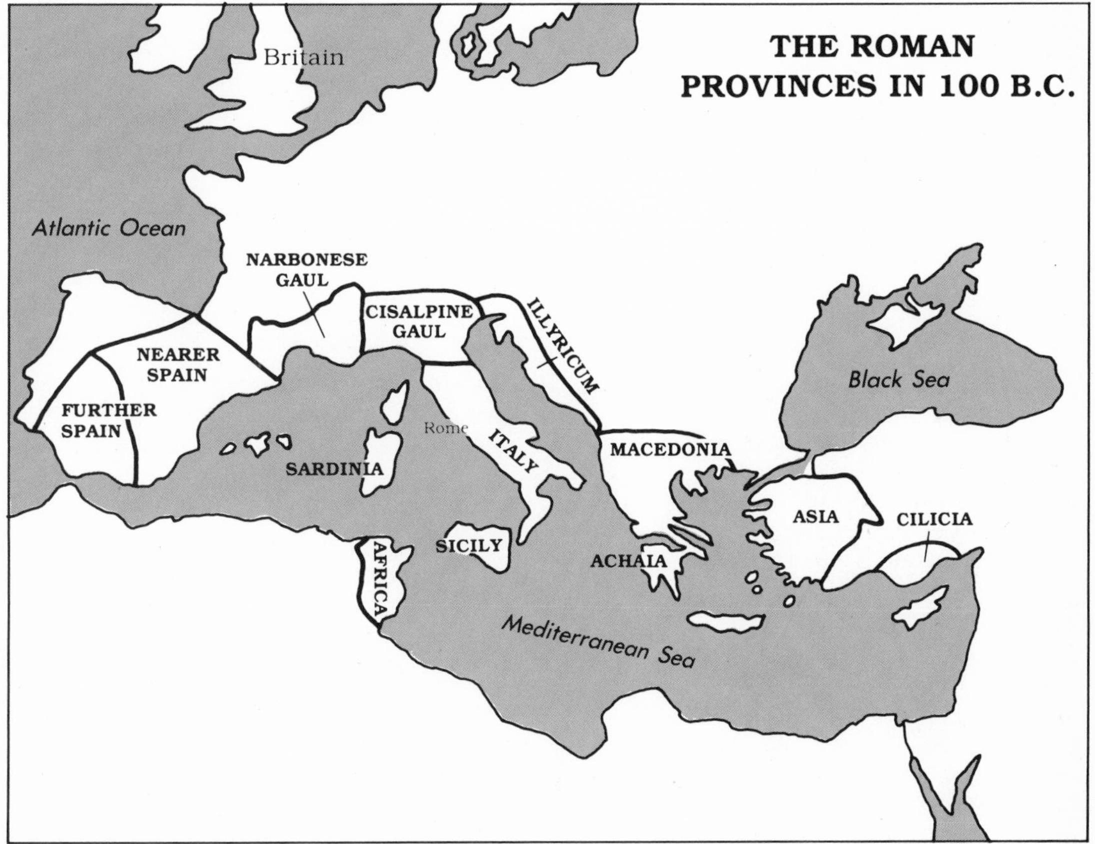

The Roman empire in 100 B.C., the year of Caesar's birth. Rome's provinces had been acquired through political alliances and military conquests and provided important revenues in the form of taxes and tributes.

their own assembly, the plebian council or *concilium plebis*, and were given officials — called tribunes — who had power to veto all government measures. By 287 B.C. plebians had won the right to serve in all high offices. Indeed, it was mandatory that one of the consuls be a plebian. Furthermore, the plebian council had been invested with the right to pass binding legislation.

By the time Caesar was born, this seemingly democratic system was dominated by a new elite composed of those Roman families who could claim consuls or other high officials as ancestors. These *nobles*, as they came to be known, exercised power through control of the Senate, the powers of which they had greatly expanded. They were linked together by marriages and supported by vast networks of less powerful Romans who were willing to offer their loyalty in exchange for material gifts and political favors. Using these networks and such methods as bribery, extortion, and intimidation, the nobles were able to determine the outcome of most consular and tribunal elections and to control most appointments to the magistracy. (The term *magistrate* referred to the consuls as well as lesser government officials possessing certain administrative and executive powers.) Only rarely did so-called new men, those without consular ancestry, attain any degree of power.

Within the Senate, rivalries often developed. Various senatorial factions produced rival candidates for elections and competed intensely for the votes of various social and economic groups. But whenever faced with a threat to their collective authority from other parts of society, the nobles tended to band together to preserve their oligarchical hold on power.

A 19th-century French painting depicts the decadence and splendor that characterized the banquets of Roman nobles. During the first century B.C. the nobility — families with ancestors who had been consuls or other high officials — dominated Roman politics through control of the Senate.

THE BETTMANN ARCHIVE

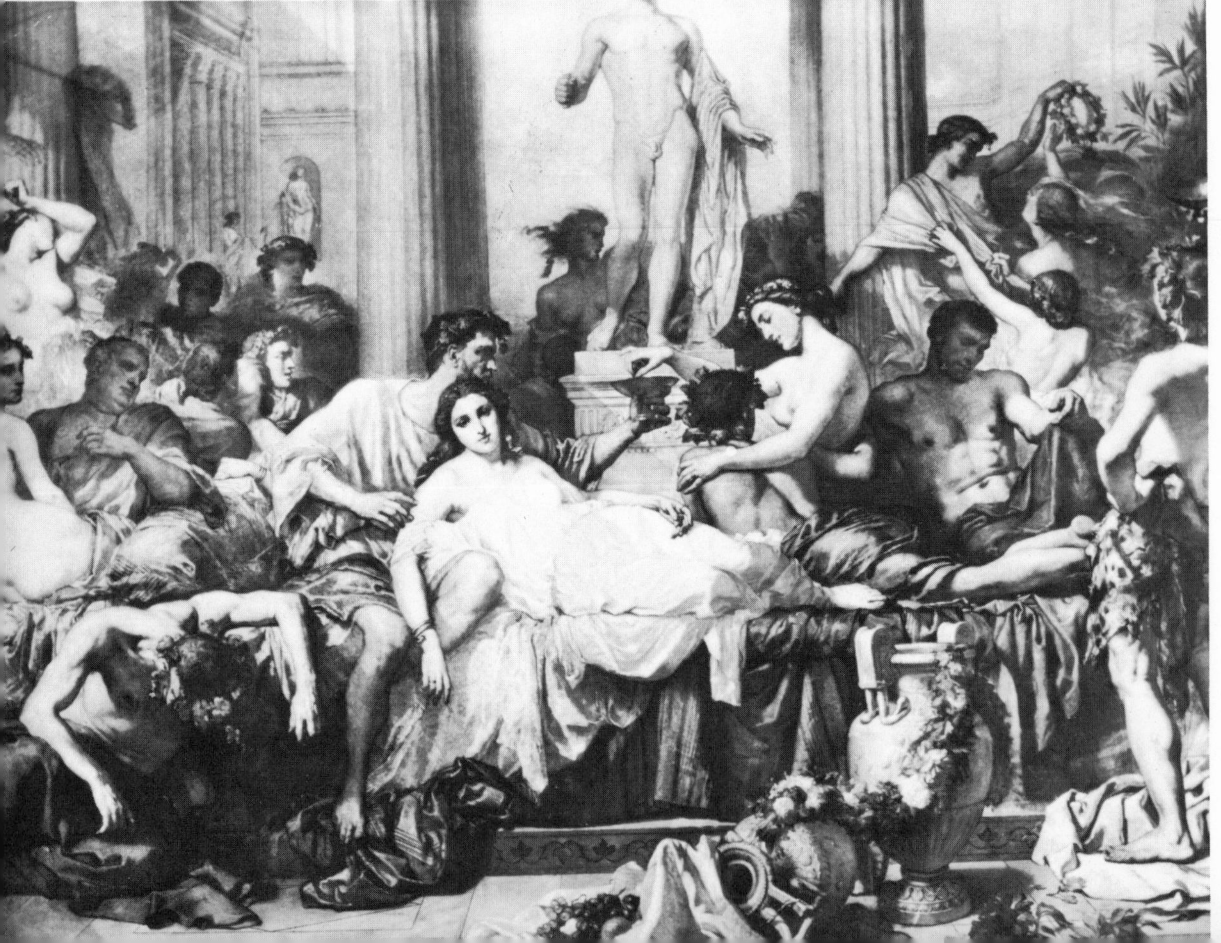

Under the leadership of the oligarchy, Rome had built a sprawling empire along the northern shore of the Mediterranean. In 100 B.C., its territory extended beyond the Italian peninsula to include the provinces of Cisalpine Gaul (present-day northern Italy), Sicily, Sardinia-Corsica, Narbonese Gaul (southern France), Illyricum (the west coast of Yugoslavia), Africa (Tunisia), Asia (western Turkey), Achaia and Macedonia (southern and northern Greece), and Cilicia (southeastern Turkey). Some of these provinces had signed treaties and were regarded as allies. Others had been subdued in brutal military campaigns and were required to pay heavy taxes or tributes. Each territory was bound to the whole by the introduction of Roman law and by the extension of Rome's dense network of finely engineered roadways. Otherwise, Rome interfered very little in its domains. Provinces were run by governors over whom the central government exercised little control.

By means of ferocious feuds and grim bargaining the nobles gathered to their support whatever social and economic groups they could, operating in conflicting, shifting gangs which expanded and disintegrated around energetic men.

—MICHAEL GRANT
British historian, on Roman politics in 100 B.C.

Provincial governors, who were chosen from the senatorial aristocracy, maintained small staffs and tended to leave the details of government to local leaders. Instead they devoted their energies to amassing personal fortunes, to recruiting regional allies whose support could prove valuable in political struggles back home, and to launching further expeditions of conquest into outlying regions.

The provinces contributed enormous riches to Rome. During conquests, it was traditional for Roman armies and their leaders to appropriate great stores of jewels, currency, clothing, armor, grain, and pottery. Once subdued, the provinces served as important sources of raw materials and as valuable markets for manufactured goods. They also provided significant opportunities for Rome's business class, the *equites* (knights or equestrians), to set up financial institutions.

Taxes from the provinces helped to fund Rome's vast, ongoing program of public works. By 100 B.C., the city featured a collection of religious and civic structures that were the envy of the ancient world. Many of these buildings were situated in the Forum, the public center where most of Rome's political, social, commercial, and religious affairs were con-

GIRAUDON/ART RESOURCE

The typical battle dress of Roman soldiers included plumed helmets with visors and wooden shields covered with leather. In Caesar's day armies were organized and funded by individual generals rather than by the state, although commands were approved by the Senate.

ducted. It was in an outdoor portion of the Forum that the assembly met for public votes and on a platform called the rostrum that important orations were delivered. The Forum's buildings included the Tabularium, the hall of records, and many temples honoring Rome's most important gods (Vesta, the goddess of home and family, and Jupiter, the ruler of the gods). There were also several columns and arches honoring Rome's war heroes. In addition to its impressive public architecture, the city boasted a water system that pumped more water per capita each year than modern New York City. The water was brought in from distant hills on long aqueducts that ran parallel to the major highways that connected Rome to its provinces.

The benefits of Rome's conquests were generally enjoyed only by the noble families. The richest ones lived in magnificent villas on hills outside of the city where frequent breezes offered relief from Rome's intense summer heat. Decorated with marble sculptures and fountains, the mansions included large libraries and luxurious baths. Each noble family owned hundreds of slaves — foreigners captured

A red clay drinking bowl from the time of Caesar shows Alexander the Great of Greece in battle against Darius III, the king of Persia. The advanced state of Roman culture in Caesar's day was partially due to Rome's exposure to Greek civilization over the preceding two centuries.

MUSEUM OF FINE ARTS, BOSTON, HENRY L. PIERCE FUND

during military conquests. Slaves served as maids, gardeners, cooks, and tutors and staffed their masters' frequent banquets. At these sumptuous feasts, guests were entertained by dancers, musicians, and acrobats while they sipped wines and sampled exotic food — including nightingale tongues and mice cooked in honey. Most Romans, however, were not wealthy. The majority lived in dilapidated tenements along dusty, narrow streets and survived on bread, olives, and wheat porridge. The city was choked with unemployed peasants who had been displaced by the rise of large, slave-manned plantations owned by the nobles.

Caesar himself was born into an aristocratic family on July 12, probably in the year 100 B.C. His full

Wealthy Romans wore delicately woven, flowing togas and rode through the streets in fine carriages. The poorer classes (facing page) wore crudely made short tunics. The growth of urban Rome brought misery and poverty for the lower classes, who were forced to live in squalid tenements.

THE BETTMANN ARCHIVE

name was Gaius Julius Caesar, also the name of his father and grandfather. The first appellation was his given name, the second his clan title, and the third a descriptive term differentiating his family within the clan. (Some historians have suggested that the cognomen Caesar might have originated when an early member of the family had to be surgically removed from the womb. In Latin, the language of the Romans, the word for womb is *caesus*.) From an early age, Caesar learned to appreciate the historical importance of his parents' clans, the Julians and the Aurelians. (Since Roman women were referred to by the feminine name of their clan, his mother was called Aurelia.) The Julian clan traced its lineage to the legendary Roman hero Aeneas, who several centuries earlier had fled the burning city of Troy as it was being overrun by the Greeks and, after an arduous journey filled with marvelous exploits, had sought refuge in Italy. The Aurelians, though they were relative "newcomers," having had their first consul around 250 B.C., boasted among their ancestors an important priest of the sun god, military heroes from Rome's conquest of Carthage two centuries earlier, and several recent consuls.

During the late second century B.C., the Julians had suffered a decline in their political power as their relatively modest fortune kept them from being able to fund great careers. Before Caesar was born, the family's position improved as a result of his aunt's marriage to Gaius Marius, the most important man of the day.

Like other noble children, Caesar was groomed almost from birth to take his place in the senatorial oligarchy. In accordance with Roman traditions, he was put in his mother's charge until the age of seven. She was to show him how to become a *vir bonus*, a good man. Most of his lessons took place inside the family's spacious, elegant home. Here, Caesar was instructed in the traditional Roman virtues. These included endurance, frugality, simplicity, religious devotion, upright dealing, and the avoidance of wrongdoing. Sitting on Aurelia's knee, Caesar heard tales of Rome's great heroes. He was taught especially to respect the achievements of his

THE BETTMANN ARCHIVE

ALINARI/ART RESOURCE

Believing that the gods controlled all aspects of life, the ancient Romans honored them with frequent sacrifices. In this frieze, Roman farmers prepare to offer up a bull and a ram. Privately skeptical about religion, in public Caesar adhered to Roman religious ritual.

uncle Marius, who was a renowned general and had been consul several times. Occasional visits to his uncle's elegant new mansion on the Palatine Hill exposed Caesar firsthand to the benefits of military conquests.

Because of Roman greed and Roman injustice, all our provinces are mourning, all our free communities are complaining, and even foreign kingdoms are protesting. As far as the bounds of Ocean there is no spot now so distant or so obscure that the wanton and oppressive deeds of Romans have not penetrated thither.
—MARCUS CICERO
Roman politician

Like most other Roman families, the Julian clan engaged in frequent rituals celebrating Rome's many deities. Every day at dawn, Caesar watched as his father threw a piece of salted cake into the fireplace as an offering to Vesta, the goddess of the hearth. Caesar himself learned to conduct a second ceremony honoring the household gods, the *lares* (spirits of the ancestors) and the *penates* (guardians of the pantry). Several times a year, the family gathered for ritual slaughters, at which Caesar's father would slit the throat of a pig or lamb with a sacred knife. Though later in life Caesar would come to view most aspects of religion as empty superstition, whenever he was asked as a public figure to perform religious rites, he would always do so with high-minded seriousness, recognizing their importance to the common people.

At the age of seven, Caesar began to attend a traditional school located in a converted shop in the heart of the commercial district. Sitting on backless benches, facing the threat of severe discipline from his teacher if he erred, Caesar was required to recite long passages of Roman and Greek prose, memorize much of the Roman legal code, and perfect the art of public speaking. At school and through frequent social contacts, Caesar developed strong friendships with other noble youths. Under his father's tutelage, he learned the intricacies of Roman politics. In 93 B.C., his father campaigned for the office of *praetor* (state judge), one of the most important positions in the Roman government. The young Caesar frequently accompanied his father to rallies and fairs where candidates solicited votes. The elder Caesar also took his son on tours of the family's large rural estates and prepared him to take over management of the family's finances someday. Such knowledge would prove useful at a much earlier age than the young Julius could have imagined at the time.

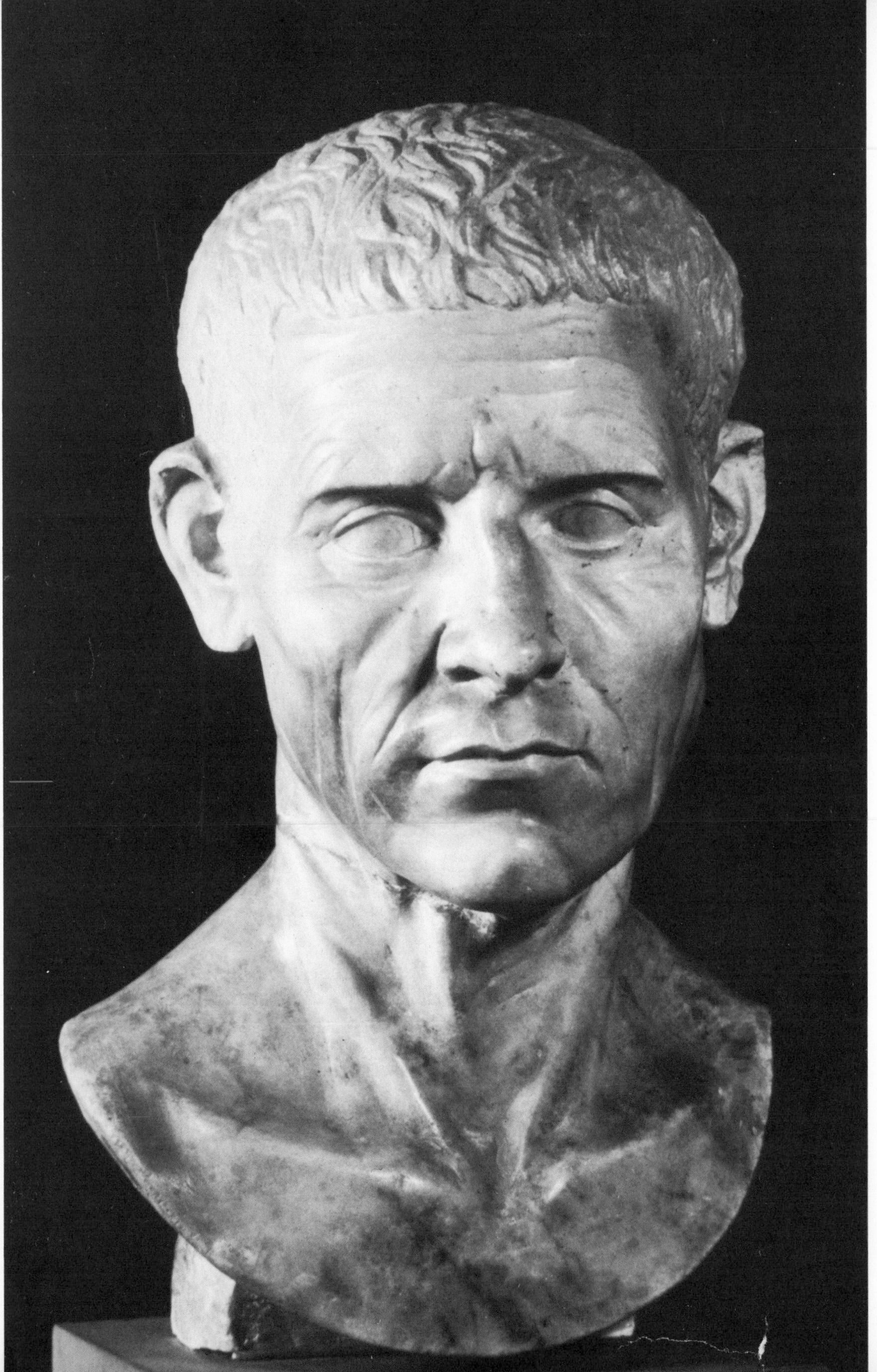

2

Toward Power

During Caesar's childhood, Roman politics became increasingly tangled and turbulent. The senatorial aristocracy's hold on power was threatened by challenges from the class below it — the equestrians — and from strong individuals in its own midst who attempted to seize autocratic control. These conflicts interrupted the normal operation of government, making it difficult for bills to be passed and programs to be implemented.

The situation was exacerbated by the gradual division of the Roman body politic into two camps, the *optimates* (literally, the "best men") and the *populares*. Though never coalescing into actual political parties, these groups reflected two general trends. Members of the populare faction tended to be in favor of bypassing the mechanism of the Senate and supported a direct appeal to the assembly and the people. In some instances, they did so out of a genuine desire to make the system more democratic, in others simply to get their own way and accumulate power and popular support for themselves. By contrast, the optimates viewed the authority of the Senate as sacrosanct. To the optimates (also known as the conservatives or diehards), the preservation of the Roman republic in its existing form — with its system of kinship, cli-

Caesar's lifetime was an era of complex struggle at Rome, more intricate than any other period of ancient history. Several times the contentions of aristocratic leaders produced bloody civil wars. The Roman Republic was dying; or to put it in less emotional terms the Romans finally had to reform their constitution to cope with their expansion abroad and changes at home in previous centuries.

—CHESTER G. STARR
modern historian

In 89 B.C. Lucius Cornelius Sulla became the first Roman general to lead an army against the government of Rome. After winning a bitter civil war, he was named dictator in 82 and ordered the execution of many of his political opponents.

SCALA/ART RESOURCE

Houseless and homeless they wander about with their wives and children. Not a man of them has an hereditary altar, not one of all these many Romans an ancestral tomb, but they fight and die to support others in wealth and luxury and though they are styled masters of the world, they have not a single clod of earth that is their own.

—TIBERIUS GRACCHUS
Roman tribune in 133 B.C., describing the Roman peasantry

entship, favor, and custom — overrode all other concerns. They carried this obsession to an extreme in passing a law (the *sentatus consultum ultimum*) that authorized, in the event of a threat to the status quo, the installment of a temporary dictator with far-reaching powers to suspend laws and to execute enemies of the state. Populares were firmly opposed to this decree but were willing to allow other, more democratic alterations of the system.

The populare approach had first been used toward the end of the previous century by the so-called Gracchi — brothers named Tiberius and Gaius Gracchus, who served as tribunes respectively in 133 B.C. and 123 B.C. Each had gone to the assembly rather than the Senate in seeking passage of legislation that would have benefitted the lower classes by redistributing public land and freezing the price of grain. Both were killed in riots started by conservatives disturbed by the direction of their reforms.

The next important populare leader was Marius, under whose guidance the populare faction gained the upper hand in Roman politics. He had less altruistic motives in appealing to the people. Marius at first encountered a great deal of resistance to his political advancement because he was the son of peasants and thus lacked consular ancestry. He was able to overcome this shortcoming and win election as consul in 107 B.C. by exploiting the support he had developed among the lower classes by virtue of his success as a military leader and earlier electoral reforms he had sponsored as tribune. As consul, he further advanced his popular appeal by succeeding in having the assembly vote him a military command in Africa, over the objections of the Senate, and successfully crushing a rebellion there. Elected consul for five straight terms from 104 B.C. to 100 B.C., he became the most powerful figure in Rome.

His position was threatened during the next decade by the rise of Lucius Cornelius Sulla. An optimate member of the Senate, Sulla attained special prominence during the Social War of 90–89 B.C., which developed when farmers inhabiting Italian regions outside Rome proper became fed up with

ALINARI/ART RESOURCE

Roman senators. During Caesar's youth, the Senate gradually split into two camps, the optimates, who supported the dominance of the Senate by the nobles, and the populares. From the beginning of his career, Caesar was associated with the populares, who tended to bypass the Senate and appeal directly to the people.

THE BETTMANN ARCHIVE

A view of Rome during Caesar's day shows a temple and lower-class tenements in the background and the Tiber River, dotted with merchant ships, in the foreground. In 80 B.C. Caesar left the city, having alienated Sulla by refusing to divorce a woman with anti-Sullan ties.

their lack of full Roman citizenship. While Sulla led successful campaigns against the peasant revolt, Marius himself was denied a military command. When Marius finally convinced the assembly to transfer Sulla's command to him, a civil war broke out. Sulla's forces marched on Rome and easily defeated those of Marius. Marius was forced into exile, and Sulla became consul for 88 B.C. Sulla soon felt obliged to lead a military expedition to Asia Minor, where Mithridates VI (the Great) of Pontus (to the northeast of the Roman province of Asia) was staging the first of several revolts he would lead against Rome during the century. In Sulla's absence Marius seized the government of Rome by force and became consul for the seventh time.

When Marius died in 86 B.C., he was quickly replaced by his ally, the celebrated general Lucius Cornelius Cinna. During this time Caesar's family, having established a strong connection to the populare faction through their marriage alliance, remained prominent. But in 85 B.C. Caesar's father died. At the age of 15 the young Caesar became head of his family. At that time, members of his clan had decided that he should pursue a religious career as a priest of Jupiter. If Caesar had followed their plan and taken such a position, he would have been forever forbidden from engaging in public life. He chose instead to dive headlong into a political career. He made his first move toward power in 84 B.C., marrying Cornelia, the daughter of Cinna, thus solidifying his own connection to the populare faction.

Caesar's career almost ended before it began. In 83 B.C. the rivalry between Rome's competing political groups took a dramatic turn. In that year Sulla returned from the east and marched again upon the government of Rome. After winning the ensuing civil war of 83–82 B.C., Sulla had himself named dictator and initiated a reign of terror in which thousands of his political opponents were killed and their property confiscated. (Marius too had been responsible for the slaughter of those he deemed his opponents.) Caesar's father-in-law, Cinna, was murdered by his own soldiers. Lists — called "proscriptions" — of enemies of the state were posted on wood tablets in the Forum. Caesar barely escaped being proscribed. He was spared only because of his youth and inexperience.

Though Sulla did not execute Caesar, he did demand that the young man, as an act of good faith to Rome's new ruler, divorce Cinna's daughter and take a wife with connections to the conservative faction. Other young Romans with blue-blooded lineages had done so, including Gnaeus Pompey (Pompey the Great), who would later become an ally and then the main rival of Caesar. Caesar brashly rejected the demand. Some historians argue that the rebuff was motivated by his tremendous love for Cornelia. Others have speculated that Caesar shrewdly recognized that Sulla's hold on Rome was tenuous and that by challenging the dictator he would endear himself to the soon-to-be ascendant rival camp. In either case, it was a risky maneuver. Cornelia's dowry was confiscated, and Caesar became worried that his life might be in danger. He soon fled Rome with several slaves to the hills of central Italy, where he lived for a time as a fugitive.

Eventually his mother's family and the priestly college of the vestal virgins won assurances from the government that Caesar could safely return — on the condition that he appear for a personal interview with the imposing dictator. For the 19-year-old Caesar, an interview with the ruthless dictator

> ***A classic counterrevolutionary, Sulla was certain that by terror he could retard, even reverse, the trend of history.***
>
> —ARTHUR D. KAHN
> modern historian

of Rome was a terrifying experience. Sulla began the encounter by criticizing the youth's physical appearance. Caesar's habit of wearing fringed sleeves to the wrist and his tendency to have his belt hanging loosely around his waist were considered strange. He also was known for taking meticulous care of his hair. Though Sulla warned that there might be many Mariuses embodied in the spirit of the young Caesar, he kept his word. Caesar left a free man.

Nevertheless, Caesar thought it was a good idea to stay out of Sulla's way for a time. Through family connections, he received an appointment on the staff of the governor of Asia. Arriving in western Anatolia, he was given, since he was a senator's son, a fairly important task. He was to travel to Bithynia, a client state of Rome's to the north of the province of Asia, to bring back a fleet of ships needed for the continuing battle against Mithridates. In Bithynia, Caesar was given a gracious welcome by King Nicomedes IV. During a banquet in his honor, Caesar made a diplomatic mistake that would haunt him for many years. Seemingly forgetting his high status as Rome's official representative, Caesar acted as Nicomedes's cupbearer during the feast. Though Caesar may have seen it as an innocent gesture of goodwill, other Romans at the banquet thought otherwise.

For a Roman noble to serve a subject of Rome's, however dignified, was considered inappropriate behavior. The gesture had other implications of which Caesar was apparently ignorant. Since Nicomedes's regular cupbearers were all youths known to be homosexual partners of the notorious king, Caesar's presence in such company made many wonder whether he too was one of the king's lovers. Although Caesar always vigorously denied having had a homosexual encounter in Bithynia, opponents would later taunt him with the charge of homosexuality. One political enemy once called Caesar "every woman's husband and every man's wife."

Caesar's next assignment in Asia was far more successful. In the Roman conquest of the city of

Mytilene, the capital of the island of Lesbos, he saw action in battle for the first time. For his efforts, he received the oak wreath, or Civic Crown, Rome's highest award for courage. It is not known exactly what he did to earn the distinction. He may have received the crown for frivolous reasons, since at that time the awarding of military honors, like most aspects of Roman society, had been corrupted. In any case, Caesar was henceforth entitled to sit next to the senators of Rome at public games. When he wore the oak wreath, all spectators, including the senators, would be obliged to rise to their feet.

In 78 B.C. Caesar received word that Sulla had died, and he decided to return to Rome. The pop-

THE BETTMANN ARCHIVE

Pictured near the end of his life, Julius Caesar wears the Civic Crown, Rome's highest award for courage. He received the distinction at the age of 20 for heroic deeds in the conquest of Mytilene. The attendant at right bears the fasces, the Roman symbol of authority.

THE BETTMANN ARCHIVE

An orator addresses the Senate. Recognizing the importance of public speaking for an aspiring politician, Caesar spent the years 78 to 75 B.C. honing his oratorical skills in the Roman courts and studying rhetoric with a famous teacher in Rhodes.

ulares, led by Marcus Lepidus, were gathering forces to attempt to drive the conservatives from power. Determining that the proposed uprising had too little support to succeed, Caesar refused to participate. Most of his energies were devoted instead to to making accusatory speeches, called prosecutions, in the Roman courts. Theoretically, any Roman could accuse another of a crime. In practice this institution was often exploited by nobles to impugn political rivals and avenge previous wrongs. To young men like Caesar, prosecutions were seen as a way to practice their oratorical skills and make themselves more widely known. Normally, their allegations were made against provincial governors, whose distance from Rome and control over areas rich in material resources made them especially prone to crimes like embezzlement. For Caesar, it was the perfect way to advance his political career, since he was known as an excellent public speaker.

In 77 B.C. Caesar charged the former governor of Macedonia, a nobleman named Gnaeus Dolabella, with having extorted money from his provincial subjects. The speech was designed not only to gain Caesar exposure but also to make him allies among the Macedonian people. In the end, Dolabella was acquitted, in part because he had undermined Caesar's credibility by reviving the controversy over Caesar's relationship with Nicomedes. But Caesar's speech had been extremely eloquent, and the text was later published for all Romans to read.

In spite of his considerable success in the courts, Caesar decided he needed additional formal training in public speaking in order to become a major figure in Roman politics. In 75 B.C. he set off for the island of Rhodes, where he was to study with the Greek rhetorician Apollonius Molon. The tutor had previously coached Marcus Cicero, a rising Roman statesman six years older than Caesar who was already establishing a reputation as one of the most impressive orators in Rome. En route to Rhodes, Caesar traveled along the coast of what is now Turkey, through an area where Roman trade had repeatedly been threatened by pirates. Caesar's vessel was captured, and he was taken hostage.

The pirates did not know quite what to make of the Roman aristocrat now in their clutches. He joked and bantered with them, scoffing at the small value of the ransom they asked for his release. The Roman historian Plutarch called these pirates "some of the most bloodthirsty people in the world," and yet Caesar acted as if they were his prisoners, not the reverse. He scolded them, telling them that after his release he would return to crucify each and every one of them. Admiring his cockiness and his utter disregard for the dangerous situation in which he was trapped, they joked back, trying to match wits with their Roman prisoner. Meanwhile, Caesar convinced local communities to raise the money the pirates had demanded.

After the ransom had been paid, the pirates released Caesar, assuming that they would never hear of him again. But soon thereafter he hired several ships, filled them with the toughest seamen he could find, and headed back to the island where he had been held prisoner. In a vicious sea battle, a substantial number of his former captors were cap-

Tall of stature, with a fair complexion, shapely limbs, a somewhat full face and keen black eyes, a long delicate neck with a prominent Adam's apple, hair slightly curling and combed forward toward the right over a high forehead, nose a trifle upturned, well-defined cheekbones within taut cheeks, a full mouth set over a sturdy chin, Caesar had the appearance as well as the bearing of a patrician.

—ARTHUR D. KAHN
modern historian

tured. Unable to convince the governor of Asia, who probably received compensation for the bandits' activities, to try them, Caesar decided independently to have them killed, and, true to his word, had them all crucified.

After his revenge against the pirates, Caesar continued his voyage. He finally arrived at the island of Rhodes to study with Molon. After he had been in Rhodes only a short time, Caesar learned that another war had broken out in the east. Mithridates had begun his third campaign against Roman troops in an effort to acquire part of Rome's Asia province.

Acting without orders from the government, Caesar quickly raised troops at his own expense, fought a successful skirmish with an advance guard of Mithridates's army, and joined the regularly appointed Roman general and his troops in preparing for the larger struggle. The final portion of Caesar's second two-year stint in Asia was spent in the ser-

In 75 B.C., while en route to Rhodes to study public speaking, Caesar was taken hostage by pirates. Pictured here aboard his captors' ship, he berates them for their impudence in seizing him and vows to seek revenge after being released.

THE BETTMANN ARCHIVE

THE BETTMANN ARCHIVE

vice of a Roman official doing battle against pirates. By 73 B.C. he had been transformed from a slight, unseasoned youth into a tough leader capable of decisive and independent action.

That year he learned that his mother's cousin Gaius Cotta, a former consul and the governor of Cisalpine Gaul, had died. Gaius's seat on the board of priests was being held for Caesar. Twenty-six years old, a veteran of wars, political upheaval, and kidnapping, a survivor, Caesar was again heading back to Rome.

Caesar assembled this battalion of Roman soldiers in 75 B.C. to combat a rebellion in the province of Asia, serving notice to Rome's leaders of his ambition and energy.

3
Emerging Politician

Caesar's position on the board of priests gave him considerable political power, since he was now entrusted with observing many of the religious rites that, according to Roman law, had to accompany all official acts. Caesar used this power to take on the optimate nobles by endorsing a plan to overturn one of Sulla's "reforms." During the former dictator's reign, the power of the tribunes had been severely restricted. The tribunes' executive and judicial powers were curtailed, and they were prohibited from ever holding other types of political office. Immediately after Sulla's death, the tribunes' right to occupy other positions was restored. Then, when Caesar took office on the board of priests, he took part in the successful effort to restore the remainder of the tribunes' powers, a process that was completed in 70 B.C. under the leadership of the consuls Pompey and Crassus. After a brief stint in the Roman army, Caesar returned to the board of priests and showed further signs of an anticonservative inclination. In his first speech before the assembly, he demanded amnesty for all anti-Sullans then living in exile.

Being at Gades [a town in Further Spain] he saw a statue of Alexander the Great and was heard to give a great sigh. It would seem that he was despondent because, at an age when Alexander had already conquered the whole world, he himself had done nothing of any importance.
—SUETONIUS
Roman historian

In 69 B.C. Caesar's aunt Julia, widow of Marius, died. Caesar asked for a ritual eulogy of his aunt, a procession through Rome of musicians, a choir,

This commemorative plate, dating from the Italian Renaissance, depicts a Roman army, including Caesar (far left), defending a provincial city against invaders. Military success was a traditional stepping-stone to power for ambitious Romans.

NIMATALLAH/ART RESOURCE

THE METROPOLITAN MUSEUM OF ART, PURCHASE ABRAHAM FOUNDATION, INC. GIFT 1978

The back of a bronze mirror from Roman times illustrates a Greek myth in which Zeus, the king of the gods, disguised himself as a bull and abducted a mortal woman named Europa. Notorious for his many love affairs, the young Caesar was extremely proud of his good looks and attractiveness to women.

and mourners. Not only was there a large crowd of people but also, in full display, a ceremonial mask of Marius, something Romans had not seen since Sulla had declared him an enemy of the state years earlier. When the procession stopped in front of the orator's platform, Caesar delivered a stirring funeral oration. To a startled crowd, he praised the virtues of his own family, descended, he asserted, from the kings of ancient Rome and the goddess Venus. He also praised the memory of Marius, Julia's husband, who had stood, he said, for the rights of all Romans. The crowd roared its approval.

To the optimates, this was quite an affront. They wondered whether this man Caesar might indeed be what Sulla had feared — a new Marius, a new leader of the opposition party. Wary of his popular support among the masses, they would now treat him with much more caution. Later in 69 B.C. Caesar's wife, Cornelia, died. Though he was known for having many extramarital affairs, Caesar had been genuinely fond of Cornelia and ordered another formal funeral procession, similar to the one given for Julia. This kind of tribute was not usually accorded

> ***Our family has at once the sanctity of kings, whose power is supreme among mortal men, and the claim to reverence which attaches to the gods, who hold sway over kings themselves.***
>
> —JULIUS CAESAR
> in a eulogy for his aunt, 69 B.C.

a woman as young as Cornelia, but Caesar honored her this way nevertheless. Most historians concur that he probably used the occasion to deliver a moving farewell to the wife of his only child, in which he also praised her father, Cinna, Gaius Marius's major ally.

Perhaps Sulla had been right when he had warned that Julius Caesar might have many Mariuses inside him. Meanwhile, the young man's considerable grace and charm won him a prominent position in the aristocratic social whirl. He was elegant and handsome, skipping from one woman's bed to another, seducing the wives of friend and enemy alike. He wore expensive clothes and preened incessantly, spent huge sums on beautiful paintings and carvings, and collected fine pearls. He mixed with the public far more than he ever had before and eagerly carried on his business at the Forum, greeting visitors with courtesy and attention. Playing the role of public servant with unusual enthusiasm and tact, offering compliments and promises of help, appearing at the marriages and funerals of all

A first-century B.C. Roman amphitheater in Spain. In 69 B.C. Caesar served as a provincial official in Further Spain, arbitrating legal disputes between local residents and forging political alliances that would prove valuable later in his career.

SCALA/ART RESOURCE

BILDARCHIV FOTO MARBURG/ART RESOURCE

Gnaeus Pompey became one of Rome's most powerful figures through success as a military commander. In 67 B.C. Caesar first established ties with Pompey by endorsing the general's candidacy for commands in the Mediterranean and Asia Minor.

classes of citizens, supporting various candidates for office, he began to amass a large political following.

At about the time of his wife's funeral, Caesar was elected as a *quaestor*, which had a term of two years. It was a position of great distinction, requiring that its 16 holders be at least 30 years old. Quaestors fulfilled a number of duties, some managing the state treasury, others working for provincial administrations. Caesar received one of the least desirable quaestorships, serving as an assistant to the governor of Further Spain (the south and southwest of present-day Spain), in charge of solving all legal disputes in the region. Despite the remote location of the colony, Caesar was able to use this post to cultivate certain friendships with local citizens that would be important later in his career. He judiciously granted favorable rulings to those who promised future support. Nevertheless, he was bored with the administrative duties of his job. The Roman historian Suetonius wrote that Caesar, noticing a statue of Alexander the Great in the Spanish city of Gades (now Cádiz), groaned as if sickened by his own worthlessness. At a similar age, Caesar lamented, Alexander had conquered the world.

Caesar left Spain after his term ended. He had a new sense of resolve. The road to power, he now realized, lay with others who already held power. He would win them over, tap into their influence and their money.

In 67 B.C. Caesar married again. This time he wed Pompeia, whose grandfathers were Sulla and a pro-Sulla consul. Caesar thought it shrewd at this time to establish ties with what had been up to now the opposite camp. His new wife's family was extremely wealthy, a fact of no small importance to Caesar, who had incurred many debts in securing his post as quaestor. Further political appointments would require the expenditure of even larger sums of money.

The great political question dominating Rome at this time concerned who was to command the Roman fleet against the increasing number of pirates plaguing the Mediterranean. The leading candidate appeared to be Pompey, who was six years older than Caesar and had enjoyed a spectacular career. A veteran military general, he had fought for Sulla against Marius's supporters in Sicily and Africa. Vain, intelligent, a great organizer, Pompey was a leading figure among the optimates (he became consul in 70 B.C.), a man Julius Caesar should by all logic have despised. Yet Caesar endorsed Pompey in the Senate for the naval position. Pompey was selected as commander in the Mediterranean and masterfully led the fleet against the pirates, clearing the sea lanes for Roman trade by the end of 67 B.C.

Pompey was then assigned the command of the Roman troops in Asia Minor, who were once again preparing to campaign against Mithridates. Caesar again gave his full support. In offering such open, generous praise of Pompey, Caesar was courting political favor, playing his political cards like a virtuoso. Caesar also began cultivating a friendship

Marcus Licinius Crassus (right), one of Rome's richest men, made Caesar his protégé. Crassus's financial backing enabled Caesar to buy the loyalty of thousands of Romans and to compete for government posts that had previously been beyond his reach.

THE BETTMANN ARCHIVE

Before thousands of cheering spectators, charioteers race at the Roman circus. Appointed in 65 B.C. as *curule aedile*, the official in charge of public works and entertainment, Caesar organized a series of lavish public games.

with Marcus Licinius Crassus, one of Rome's wealthiest men. "Nobody can afford to become a force in politics," Crassus once said, "unless he can support a private army." Crassus could support a private army and much, much more. He was, indeed, a strong force in Roman politics, becoming consul, with Pompey, in 70 B.C. Crassus had made his fortune in inventive ways. He once bribed the city's fire brigade to allow buildings to burn until the owners sold them to him for ludicrously low prices, and he made huge profits in speculation on the property of Sulla's victims during the time of his dictatorship.

If a successful political career depended to a large extent on the control of large sums of money, there was no better way for the debt-ridden Caesar to increase his influence than to align himself with Crassus. Caesar soon became Crassus's right-hand man. He helped Crassus to manage his many business interests, which ranged from silver mines to slave trading. Much to Crassus's dismay, Caesar

THE BETTMANN ARCHIVE

even took an interest in the rich man's wife, Tertulla.

In 65 B.C. Caesar, with the financial help of his new ally Crassus, won the office of *curule aedile*, the official in charge of buildings, streets, sanitation, and the public games. It was a political position from which he was able to greatly influence public opinion.

At the state's expense, Caesar regularly organized extravagant games that drew thousands of people. The contests were especially popular among the poor, who welcomed diversion from the daily grind of poverty. Perched on several tiers of stone benches, the crowds would cheer for charioteers, who raced horse-drawn two-wheeled carts around the arena at spectacular speeds. The chariots would often smash together, their locked wheels sending out a shower of sparks.

The Roman masses also thrilled to the games of the gladiators — slaves or condemned criminals trained in special schools to fight each other to death in the arena. Armed with shields and swords or with nets and tridents, they fought to the cheers and taunts of the enormous crowd. The clash of steel, the disfiguring of bodies, the screams of the vanquished, brought thunderous roars. For the winners it meant a small reward — palm branches — and the right to fight again; for the losers it usually meant death. The wounded would plead for mercy from the president of the games. Those who had fought with bravery and skill might be spared; the timid and fearful were always executed.

The people of Rome loved the games. For Julius

A Roman gladiator looks triumphantly toward the crowd after killing all of his opponents. As Caesar's extravagant spending on public games earned him tremendous support from the lower classes, suspicious senators passed a law limiting the number of gladiators he could employ.

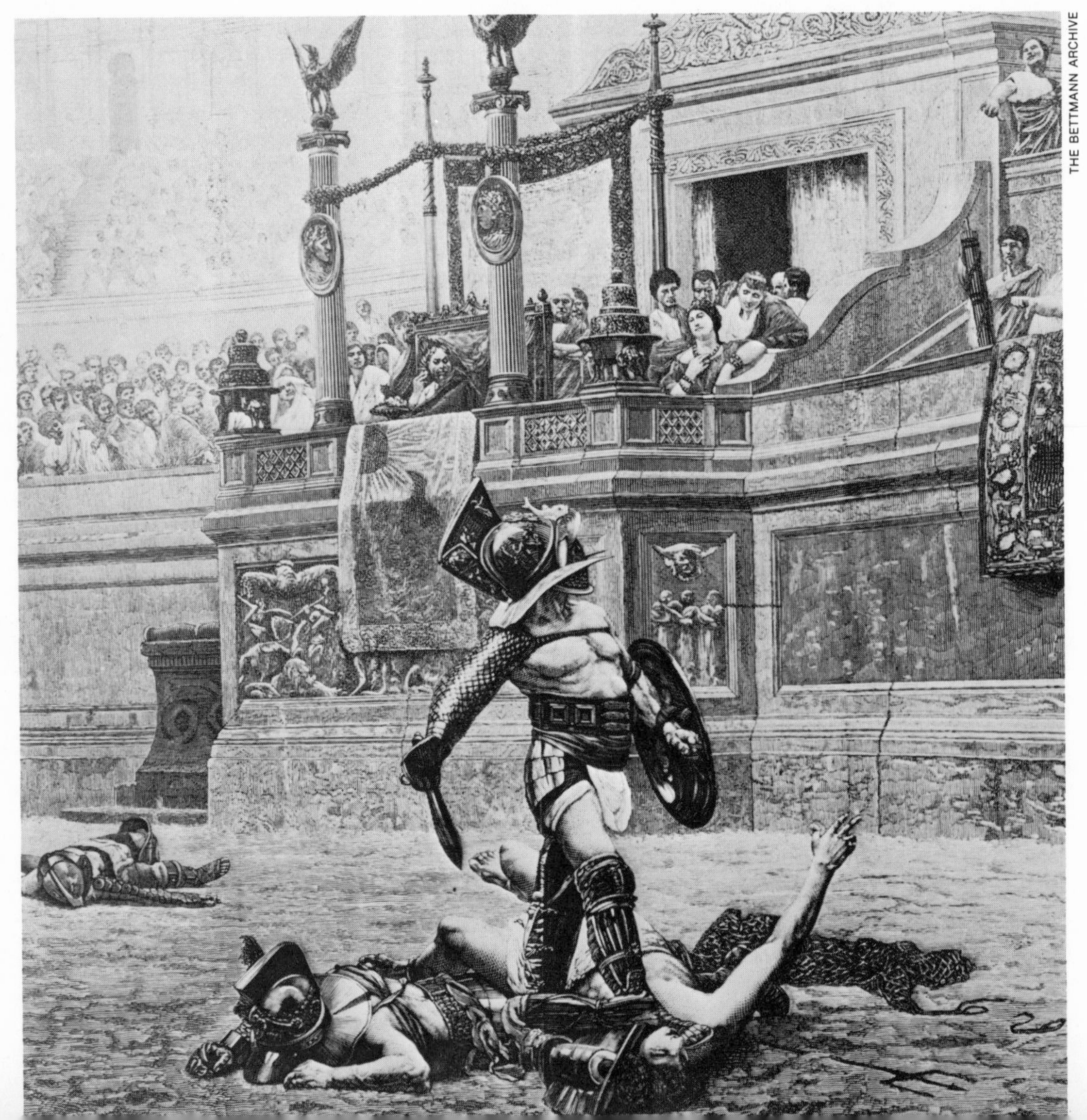

THE BETTMANN ARCHIVE

Caesar, his position was an unmatched opportunity to increase his public support. He spent more money on the games than anyone had ever spent before. He recruited so many gladiators for a series of games in 65 B.C. that the Senate, fearing that he was up to some devious purpose, put a limit on the number that could participate. Caesar equipped the gladiators with flashy silver armor, decorated public buildings and squares with colorful bunting, even sponsored stage plays and organized a wild beast hunt. He approved an unprecendented number of processions and public feasts. As a result, many citizens were willing to support Caesar in an election.

> ***Throughout his career, out of respect for tradition and out of antiquarian interest, he [Caesar] honored religious beliefs and practices although disowning divine influence in his own activity.***
> —ARTHUR D. KAHN
> modern historian

As Caesar's popularity among the citizens increased, his confidence swelled. When the chief priest, or *pontifex maximus*, of Rome died in 63 B.C., Caesar considered his own chances of winning an election to fill the office. The position was usually reserved for a man who had served many years in the Senate or the military. Two respectable political figures had already declared their candidacies. Nevertheless, Caesar, emboldened by his growing support among the people, announced that he would run for the office. It was a reckless, daring gamble. To win would mark him as perhaps Rome's most exciting young politician; to lose would be a complete humiliation.

Caesar spent huge sums of money on the election. He hired scores of workers to paint election posters on the sides of buildings to tell voters of his concern for their rights and welfare. The unconvinced were bribed. On the day of the election, Caesar told his mother that she should not expect to see him again if he lost; he had borrowed so much money that a loss would force him to flee Rome to escape death at the hands of his creditors. Incredibly, Caesar won the election by a large majority. He now settled down in the palatial estate provided the chief priest, near the Forum. He was a man of power.

4

The Triumvirate

> ***All men who deliberate upon difficult questions ought to be free from hatred and friendship, anger and pity.***
>
> —JULIUS CAESAR during a senatorial debate over the Catiline conspiracy

Caesar had shaken the political foundation of Rome, effectively challenging the conservative nobility's dominance of government. As he took office the optimates were beginning to take notice of his growing influence.

In 63 B.C. a political crisis shook Rome. One of the candidates for the two consulships was a man named Catiline. At one time a henchman of Sulla's, Catiline was now regarded with suspicion by the optimates, having amassed huge debts and become disarmingly erratic in his behavior. After a term as governor of Africa, he had suffered an embarrassing prosecution. In 65 B.C., he was reputed to have been involved in a conspiracy to assassinate Rome's consuls and replace them with two notoriously corrupt officials. At the time rumors circulated linking Crassus and Caesar to the plot, but these were probably unfounded. As controversy over the plot subsided, Caesar and his benefactor agreed to donate funds to keep Catiline's career alive, hoping to win him over to the anticonservative cause by creating a debt of gratitude.

In the election of 63 B.C. Catiline faced Gaius Hybrida and the increasingly powerful Cicero. Cicero was a "new man," so called because none of his ancestors had been a member of the ruling aristocracy. Nevertheless, he and Hybrida received the sup-

Caesar's rise to power was made possible by his prowess as a military commander, his ability to gather popular support, and his use of shrewd political alliances. In 60 B.C. he wrested power from the oligarchy by joining with Crassus and Pompey to form the First Triumvirate.

ALINARI/ART RESOURCE

port of the conservative nobles, who were disturbed by Catiline's revolutionary leanings. In spite of the apparent endorsement of Crassus and Caesar, Catiline lost the election. He began to plot the violent overthrow of the government in response.

Since Catiline had many enemies, news of his plot quickly leaked to Roman politicians. When Caesar and Crassus got wind of it, they passed the information on to Cicero, attempting to distance themselves from their former ally; Cicero had already received a full account of the plot from his mistress. In an emotionally charged, bitter harangue on the Senate floor, which became a model of superlative Latin oratory to future generations, Cicero called for the arrest of Catiline and his fellow conspirators. Most of Catiline's men were soon apprehended and thrown in jail. Catiline himself fled from Rome.

As the Senate met to consider the fate of the prisoners, Caesar was in a difficult position. Catiline's enemies, principally Cicero, were also his own ene-

Though a "new man" (not of aristocratic parentage), Marcus Cicero was a relentless defender of the Roman oligarchy. The greatest philosopher, writer, and orator of his day, Cicero was elected consul in 63 B.C. and clashed with Caesar over the Catiline conspiracy.

mies. To attack Catiline would be to attack many of his own supporters. To rise to the defense of Catiline, however, would be to condone assassination plots and other treasons.

In December 63 B.C. the Senate debated the Catiline conspiracy. When several senators demanded that all of the prisoners be put to death, Caesar took a sensible middle position. He pointed out that the death penalty was illegal under Roman law. If the senators took it upon themselves to ignore this law, he argued, all laws would be threatened. Instead, he recommended life imprisonment.

Caesar's pleas went unheeded. Led by the furious attacks of Cicero and another senator, Cato of Utica (known also as Cato the Younger), a staunch conservative, the Senate ordered the execution of the prisoners. Catiline died in exile shortly thereafter. Some historians suggest that he was killed; others say that he committed suicide. The conspiracy was thus destroyed, a rousing victory for Cicero and Cato. However, in destroying Catiline, they had not been able to destroy Caesar.

The Catiline conspiracy had further galvanized Roman political forces into two sharply divided camps. It had also greatly enhanced the reputation of Cicero, who, though not closely aligned with either party, had become an uncompromising foe of Caesar's. Meanwhile Pompey was due soon to return from the east. By virtue of his military and political successes, Pompey had the power and support to alter the constantly shifting balance of power in Rome. Rome, and Caesar, warily awaited his arrival.

In 62 B.C. Caesar was elected praetor, a state judge. A praetorship was a prestigious position, awarded to only eight individuals each term. Each praetor was guaranteed, after his year of service, a provincial governorship, which brought with it myriad opportunities to amass a personal fortune (spoils from additional conquests, taxes on constituents, gifts). For Caesar, it was a golden opportunity to escape from debt and to acquire a large enough stake to escape Crassus's shadow and become a power in his own right. Caesar was now chief priest,

THE METROPOLITAN MUSEUM OF ART

A bronze figure of a Roman orator. Oratory was an important facet of Roman political life. Known as an excellent public speaker, Caesar used, according to one historian, "pure, plain language and a somewhat high-pitched delivery accompanied by vigorous gesticulation."

SCALA/ART RESOURCE

Speaking before the Senate in 63 B.C., Cicero accuses Catiline (seated alone at right) of conspiring to overthrow the Roman state. Catiline fled Rome, but his coconspirators were arrested and — despite Caesar's advocacy of life imprisonment — executed.

a praetor, and a member of the Senate. Senatorial battles, many of them involving Caesar, began to assume an even more ominous shape. As Caesar and his adversaries bitterly struggled over almost every issue, Rome became the scene of many mass protests and riots. Politicians were attacked and sometimes injured. Caesar was threatened by sword-wielding thugs in the Senate. Cato left one meeting battered and bleeding. Roman government, inflamed by the passion of its leaders, was rapidly disintegrating into mob rule.

Late in 62 B.C. the familiar scent of scandal again encircled Julius Caesar. This time the whispers heard around Rome did not concern Caesar's own behavior but rather that of his wife. Every year a feast honoring *Bona Dea*, the "Good Goddess," was held in the house of one of Rome's leading women. The feast contained several traditions handed down from antiquity; for instance, to preserve the rustic flavor of the event, wine was referred to as honey and the wine jar as a honey pot. Though most noble families did not place stock in such symbolism, the ritual was maintained, primarily as an opportunity for lighthearted revelry. (Women were reported to get extremely drunk at the feast.) The strictest rule was that only women could participate. Caesar's wife Pompeia, chosen to preside over the secret rites of the ceremony, secretly invited a lover of hers, a

> *Of all these things respecting which learned men dispute there is none more important than clearly to understand that we are born for justice, and that right is founded not in opinion but in nature.*
>
> —MARCUS CICERO

young man named Publius Clodius, to the festivities. Clodius entered the home dressed as a woman. He was quickly discovered by a female slave when he forgot to disguise his voice. The alarmed women at the feast drove the overwhelmed Clodius into the streets.

Roman society fluttered with excitement. Worried that the affair might damage his political reputation and upset that he had suffered public humiliation, Caesar immediately divorced his wife. Since there was obviously no emotional bond between them and since Pompeia was no longer politically useful, Caesar considered her expendable. It was at this time that he uttered his famous phrase "Caesar's wife must be above suspicion!" Caesar's opponents would not let the scandal die easily. To further embarrass Caesar, the conservatives brought Clodius, a rising politician in his own right, to trial for blasphemy. During the proceedings, Pompeia's young lover was additionally accused of committing incest with his sisters, prompting heated exchanges on the Senate floor. Cicero, who reportedly had competed with Clodius for the same mistress, led the assault on the young man's reputation. For his part, Caesar refused to testify against his cuckolder, cynically concluding that Clodius might prove a useful ally in the future.

In 61 B.C. Caesar assumed office as governor of Further Spain and, unleashed from the political snares and intrigues in Rome, seemed rejuvenated. He proved himself an able administrator and led successful military campaigns that won Rome new territory. He was well liked by his troops. He slept in the open with them, shared their food, marched with them through the mountain passes. At the end of each conquest, Caesar rewarded himself with a large share of the spoils.

In 60 B.C. Caesar returned to Rome determined to win for himself the consulship. With the hostility between Caesar and the optimate leaders still as intense as ever, he began to look for a way to combat the conservatives' hold on Roman political power.

For many years Caesar had carefully cultivated friendships with Pompey and Crassus. Now he

A bronze statuette of Fortuna, a patron goddess of Rome; she represented the unpredictable nature of fate. In 62 B.C., Caesar's fortunes swung wildly, as he was first elected to the prestigious post of praetor and then embarrassed by a public scandal involving his wife's lover.

THE METROPOLITAN MUSEUM OF ART, PURCHASED BY SUBSCRIPTION, 1896.

asked them to join forces with him in a coalition to wrest control of the Roman government from the entrenched nobility.

Pompey had returned to Rome the triumphant hero of his campaigns in the east, where, under his command, Mithridates had finally been defeated and new possessions had been added to Rome's empire. He had not been welcomed with open arms by Cicero, Cato, and the other politicians who were jealous of his successes and fearful of his power. He was angry and bitter and ready to work with Caesar. Crassus, despite his wealth, had also seen his power slip away to the optimates. He too was ready to join forces, despite his jealousy of Pompey, which dated to a dispute over the proper distribution of credit for military successes the two had achieved in quelling an earlier slave rebellion. Thus was formed the First Triumvirate (a word — *triumvirate* — derived from a Latin phrase meaning "three men").

To fortify the alliance, Caesar arranged to have his daughter, Julia, marry Pompey; Caesar himself took as his third wife Calpurnia, the daughter of one of Pompey's friends. The triumvirate began to dominate Roman politics. Blending Pompey's legendary military reputation and loyal political follow-

Merchants, acrobats, soldiers, and senators fill the open area of the Forum, the center of political, religious, and commercial affairs in Rome.

THE BETTMANN ARCHIVE

ing with Caesar's own growing body of supporters and Crassus's huge fortune, the triumvirate became an imposing force.

Caesar was elected consul in 59 B.C. and quickly showed a natural gift for pushing through legislation. He won passage of a series of measures that were extremely popular with the Roman people and thus brought great honor to the triumvirate. These included a bill providing free land for Pompey's veterans who had fought in the Far East, a bill requiring the government to refund some of the taxes levied against a number of Crassus's friends, and a bill to ease the terrible congestion of the city by making additional rural land available for the poor.

After strengthening his hold on Rome through legislative successes, Caesar proceeded to use his position as consul to chip away at the power of political opponents. He managed to have the dangerous Cato assigned to the governorship of the distant island of Cyprus, from which distance he would have difficulty hurling his legendary insults at Caesar. Soon another longtime foe of Caesar would also be forced to leave Rome. In 59 B.C., Cicero found himself involved in an acrimonious feud with Clodius, whom the distinguished orator had castigated three years earlier for his involvement in the Bona Dea scandal. Clodius had never forgotten and now, having become a tribune and a vigorous backer of Caesar, yearned for revenge.

At first merely a verbal battle, the controversy soon took on a more sinister air. Clodius hired a group of thugs to harass Cicero and his servants everywhere they went. On the streets, at his home, in the Senate, the thugs made Cicero's life miserable. When the intimidation became unbearable, Cicero went into exile, a depressed, defeated man.

Julius Caesar and his two allies, Pompey and Crassus, controlled Rome. The triumvirate, however, was a loose, uncertain alliance between three men of huge ego and ambition. It remained to be seen whether the three could work together as a stable governing force, or whether the triumvirate would break apart as one or the other sought to seize individual power, igniting more political war.

THE BETTMANN ARCHIVE

The standard that accompanied all Roman armies. "SPQR" is an abbreviation of *Senatus Populusque Romanus*, a Latin phrase meaning "The Senate and the People of Rome."

5

Gaul

Ambitious and confident, Caesar was not content with being a mere consul. The ruler of Rome, he realized, had to be a military conqueror. The next stop on his drive for glory would be the land of Gaul.

No man ever made war so horribly as Caesar did in Gaul.
—BERNARD MONTGOMERY
modern British general

Except for a small amount of action in Asia Minor and Spain, Caesar had little experience commanding troops. Caesar, now in his middle forties, was launching a major military campaign, one that might require several years to complete. But he was a man of prodigious energy and endurance and, especially at this time in his life, a man with great determination and purpose.

Northern Gaul consisted of large expanses of unconquered land, which seemed to Caesar destined for Roman control. Only the region's many independent tribes stood in the way of capturing this territory.

In 58 B.C. Caesar had himself assigned proconsul, or provincial governor, of Illyricum, Cisalpine Gaul, and Narbonese (or Transalpine) Gaul (a large area bounded by the Rhine River, the Atlantic Ocean, the Pyrennees and Alps mountains, and the Mediterranean Sea). Much of the land was raw and unknown. Caesar's term of office was for five years, time enough, he thought, to appropriate the wealth of that land, both for Rome and for himself.

It was a superbly disciplined, highly trained

Caesar in middle age. In 59 B.C. he used his position as consul to secure the governorship of Illyricum, Cisalpine Gaul, and Transalpine Gaul for the next five years.

BILDARCHIV FOTO MARBURG/ART RESOURCE

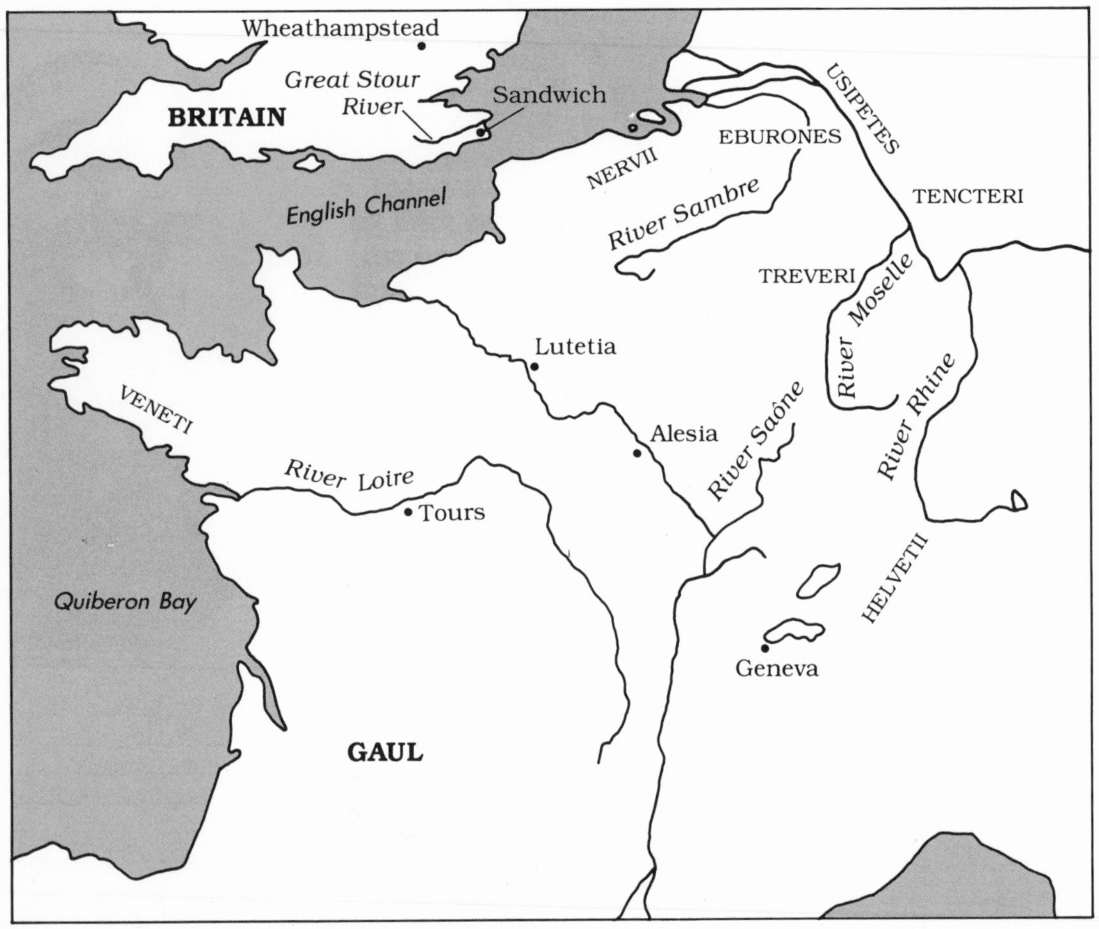

A map of Gaul, where from 58 to 51 B.C. Caesar waged campaigns against the nomadic tribes that inhabited the regions. His military success there translated itself into increased political power in Rome.

professional army that Caesar led into Gaul. The troops were an impressive sight — their colorful battle colors carried by the standard-bearers; their horn blowers blaring out the battle signals; their one-hundred-men units, the centuries, in careful, precise drill, led by their officers, the centurions, with their gleaming golden helmets crested by plumes; their powerful legions made up of 60 centuries of 6,000 men; their battle gear of iron and leather tunics, iron helmets with flaps to protect the sides of their faces, heavy leather shields, eight-foot javelins, and short-bladed swords. Army engineers built forts, laid out roads, and repaired the weapons. Mercenaries, hired soldiers from other countries, joined the Roman force — cavalry from Spain and Germany and archers from Egypt. The Roman armies, with their organization and discipline, were the most formidable in the world.

Conquering Gaul had long been a Roman objective because of the constant nuisance posed by regular incursions of its warrior tribes into Italy. With long mustaches and shaggy hair, wearing full-length trousers, members of these tribes seemed barbarous to the clean-shaven, tunic-clad Romans. The Greek historian Diodorus Siculus left behind lengthy descriptions of Gallic warriors. The Gauls, wrote Diodorus, sported helmets adorned with horns, massive gold armbands, and body-length shields decorated with paintings of wild beasts. "They [the Gauls] appear very threatening," Diodorus wrote, "yet they have sharp wits and are often clever in learning." Their confidence in life after death reportedly endowed them with great courage in battle.

In March 58 B.C., as Caesar mobilized his army, a Celtic tribe called the Helvetii, a band of nearly

GIRAUDON/ART RESOURCE

A Gallic warrior (right) raises his sword against a Roman soldier. Although the Gauls' long hair and fierce conduct in battle made them seem barbaric to Romans, Gallic civilization boasted significant achievements in agriculture, metallurgy, pottery, and public speaking.

400,000 men, women, and children, were reported to be on the move, leaving their home on the north shore of Lake Geneva, in what is now Switzerland, and crossing Transalpine Gaul to the Atlantic Ocean. The army of Caesar would thus see early action. Caesar confronted the Helvetii at Bibracte, west of the Saône River, near present-day Autun, France. The Helvetii attempted to tell Caesar that they were not there to fight the Romans but to move their people farther west, away from marauding bands of Germanic tribes that had been disrupting their lives. Caesar listened to their pleas but refused to allow them passage. If the Helvetii wanted to move west, they would have to defeat the Roman army. The two sides prepared for battle. While Rome had the advantage in organization and superior weaponry, the Helvetii had a far larger army.

Wheeling into a close-grouped battle formation, the Helvetii charged the Roman lines. They were met by a deadly volley of javelins that cut down the first line of troops. Perfectly timing their counterattack, Caesar's men charged the Helvetii, producing a

A relief sculpture of a Roman cavalry soldier. Caesar's cavalry was to prove itself invaluable in the fierce fighting that accompanied his utter subjugation of Gaul.

ALINARI/ART RESOURCE

heavy death toll with their slashing swords. Confused and panicked, the Helvetii retreated behind a small hill, where they regrouped and launched another furious charge against one of the Roman flanks.

Luck is the greatest power in all things, especially in war. Luck can be given a helping hand.
—JULIUS CAESAR

With almost mechanical precision, Caesar's men mowed down the attackers, this time causing the surviving Helvetii to swing back in a desperate, frantic retreat. Women and children were forced to join the battered remnants of the Helvetii army in a mad, wild stampede for safety. Caesar's troops methodically pursued them. The Roman cavalry hunted down the Helvetii and, throughout the late afternoon, butchered thousands.

As news of Caesar's victory spread throughout Gaul, the leaders of several tribes traveled to Roman headquarters to offer congratulations. Most of them assured Caesar that they themselves wanted peace. Some came to ask for his help against their enemies. One leader, however, was unimpressed by Caesar's slaughter of the Helvetii, and he brazenly challenged the Romans. Ariovistus, a German chieftain, arrogantly claimed to be the strongest man in Gaul, asserting that his army would smash the Roman invaders. Caesar was enraged by the man's insolence.

Caesar's soldiers were not eager to fight against the forces of Ariovistus, having heard stories of the great physical size of the German fighters. Caesar wandered among his legions, rebuking them for their lack of confidence in their own prowess and their faithlessness in his generalship. About fifteen miles from the Rhine River, near the fortress at Vesontio (now Besançon), Caesar's forces, again badly outnumbered, met the Germans. It was a bloody, chaotic battle, fought mostly hand to hand — a momentous clash of men and arms that left thousands dead. In the end, the Germans finally yielded, running for the safety of the Rhine.

With these two military victories Caesar had subdued a large part of Gaul. No army now ventured forth to test Roman power. Caesar spent the winter of 58–57 B.C. in Burgundy. Then, in 57 B.C., he added to his conquests by easily defeating a Belgic

The enemy recognized my scarlet cloak, and then saw my combined force moving down the slope.

—JULIUS CAESAR
in his book
The Gallic Wars

tribe called the Nervii who had threatened Roman dominance of Gaul by stockpiling arms.

Back in Rome, news was trickling in about Caesar's successes. Romans were fascinated by stories of the unknown tribes and towns, the new world that Caesar was winning for Rome. Some of the spoils of Caesar's remarkable triumphs — human slaves, elaborate gold carvings, silver-decorated swords and daggers, and gem-studded collars and shoulder clasps — were returned to Rome. Caesar's conquests also brought the promise of new opportunities for Roman citizens — new jobs in Gaul, new land, a chance for wealth.

Reacting to the public mood, the Roman Senate in 57 B.C. declared a public thanksgiving of fifteen days to celebrate the triumphant achievements of the conqueror. This was the longest thanksgiving ever held, five days longer than that ordered for Pompey on his return from the East.

Even Cicero applauded Caesar's victories. An end to Cicero's exile had been engineered by Pompey, who was anxious to establish a closer relationship

The Germanic chieftain Ariovistus (left) tells Caesar that the Roman army has no authority in Gaul. Caesar responded with an attack in 58 B.C. that left most of Ariovistus's 120,000 men dead.

THE BETTMANN ARCHIVE

As shown in this engraving, some Germanic tribes in Gaul recruited women for their armies. By the fall of 57 B.C., Caesar's spectacular victories in Gaul had earned him tremendous renown in Rome.

with the great orator, to take advantage of his considerable political following. Cicero, one of Julius Caesar's most consistent antagonists, a man who had doggedly attacked Caesar's every political move, was now praising the Gallic triumphs. It was a supreme irony.

As Caesar's military reputation grew, his political standing began to suffer. In late 57 B.C. petty jealousies and disputes among members of the triumvirate weakened the alliance. Though Pompey had been instrumental in gaining official recognition of Caesar's triumphs, as time went on, he began to resent his fellow triumvir; Caesar's victories in Gaul threatened to outshine his own celebrated conquests in Asia. At the same time, Caesar worried that his prolonged absence from Rome might enable Pompey to accumulate disproportionate power, particularly since Pompey had recently won a prestigious appointment as the head of a commission assigned to remedy massive grain shortages in Rome. Control over food supplies made Pompey especially important in the eyes of the people. The already shaky relationship between Crassus and Pompey deteriorated further when the latter charged repeatedly that the former had plotted to have him assassinated.

The conservatives took advantage of dissension in the opposite camp to elect in 56 B.C. a consul who strongly opposed the triumvirate. The great orator Cicero also capitalized on the situation, abandoning his promise to support the triumvirate, which he had made when Pompey facilitated his return from exile. In early 56 B.C., he rose before the Senate and attacked the constitutionality of Caesar's provincial assignment. By April, Caesar, Crassus, and Pompey finally recognized the importance of their alliance and agreed to meet to settle their differences. They came together at Luca, a quiet village on the border between Italy and Cisalpine Gaul. After a few days of bargaining, they concluded a secret pact. As the first stage of their scheme, it was decided, Crassus and Pompey were to secure election as consuls. Once installed, the two were to seek passage of a law that would extend Caesar's command in Gaul by five years and grant military commands to Crassus (in Syria) and Pompey (in Spain). This agreement renewed and solidified the triumvirate. Caesar left Luca with fresh enthusiasm, confident that his political future was again secure.

Caesar had returned to his winter quarters in Cisalpine Gaul, convinced that he had succeeded in pacifying most of Gaul in 57 B.C. During the winter he learned that the Veneti, a tribe living on the coast of Brittany, had revolted against the Roman occupation there. They had taken hostage several Roman officials who had attempted to appropriate local supplies of corn and had also gained the support of many other tribes in western Gaul. After the Luca meeting, as the rebellion grew, Caesar quickly marched his army to the Atlantic coast.

At first the Veneti, a noted seafaring people, successfully avoided an encounter with the Romans by withdrawing to their coastal towns, which were protected by steep cliffs and roaring surf. The only way to engage the Veneti, Caesar decided, would be to fight them at sea. He ordered his men to return to the Loire valley, where they constructed a flotilla of ships. The vessels were light, oar-driven galleys, each featuring several towers to accommodate archers. In contemplating a naval attack on the Veneti, Caesar was playing into the tribe's strength.

Naturally some of his men doubted the wisdom of this strategy. Their concern increased after the Veneti easily defeated Rome in the first battles at sea. The Veneti appeared to have far superior technology. Powered by durable sails, the Veneti's massive barges were built to ride high in the water and thus could navigate shallow inlets where the Roman galleys' deep hulls prevented them from going. Eventually, however, the Romans developed their own ingenious technology. Taking thin wooden poles and attaching metal hooks to the end, they created a tool with which they could dismantle the rigging of enemy vessels. In a climactic battle in Quiberon Bay, the Romans' use of this device along with a temporary lull in the wind left Veneti ships dead in the water. Veneti sailors sat helpless as Roman troops surrounded and captured their ships. Caesar ordered the Veneti leaders executed and the remainder of the population sold into slavery. It was a warning to any other tribes in Gaul that might be contemplating a similar rebellion.

Back in Rome, Crassus and Pompey harnessed their enormous combined resources to implement the Luca plan. First, in mid-56 B.C., they announced that they intended to run for the consulships of 55 B.C. When an incumbent consul charged that they had not announced their candidacies early enough to be considered, Crassus and Pompey bribed an official to delay the vote until the end of the year, when the objections of the consul would no longer carry any weight. Their victory at the polls was guaranteed by 1,000 soldiers loaned from Caesar's army. Upon taking office, they instituted the law that they had conceived at Luca. It was called the *lex Pompeia Licinia*. Then Pompey and Crassus both hastened to raise armies for their commands in Syria and Spain.

In 55 B.C. Caesar left his winter quarters in Cisalpine Gaul earlier than usual, anxious for new adventures on the other side of the Alps. His destination was the Rhine River, the boundary between the Celtic and Belgic tribes of the south and west and the German tribes of the east and north. He had received word that two German bands, the Usipetes and Tencteri, had reportedly crossed the river and were migrating southward, disrupting Gallic tribes as they went. Upon finally catching up to the two groups, Caesar was at first uncharacteristically generous, offering the Germans a treaty that would cede them land already belonging to a

THE BETTMANN ARCHIVE

A Gallic leader's valiant last stand against Roman troops illustrates the enormous carnage that typified Caesar's campaigns in Gaul. His brutal massacre of two Germanic tribes in 55 B.C. enraged his political opponents in Rome.

tribe that was an ally of Rome. As further negotiations proceeded, however, a small skirmish somehow broke out between the Roman and German cavalries. The Germans, who were greatly overmatched, made quick work of their more powerful counterparts. An enraged Caesar demanded an apology. When a German delegation arrived at his camp, Caesar decided not to forgive them. Instead, he ordered the petitioners to be executed and commanded his army to attack the rest of the German forces and the civilians who had accompanied them across the Rhine. What ensued was bloodletting on a scale difficult to imagine. After completely annihilating the German army, the Romans set upon their women and children, who scattered in several directions, running for their lives. In Caesar's words, "When they reached the confluence of the Moselle and the Rhine, they realized that they could flee no farther. A large number was killed, and the rest plunged into the water and perished, overcome by the force of the current in their terror-stricken and exhausted state." By Caesar's account the Romans had killed nearly half a million people; not a single Roman soldier had died.

A frieze adorning a Roman sarcophagus, or stone coffin, depicts a battle between Romans and Germans. In 55 B.C. Caesar crossed from Gaul over the Rhine River, a symbolic gesture aimed at stemming German incursions.

SCALA/ART RESOURCE

The massacre was so brutal that it even offended the cynical, hard-hearted senators of Rome. In contrast to the thanksgivings that Caesar had received for earlier conquests, he now was charged with barbarism and inhumanity. Cato demanded that Caesar be handed over to the Germans to atone for his misdeeds. Otherwise, Cato argued, the whole of Rome would incur the wrath of the gods. Of course, the proposal was motivated by political considerations as well as religious ones; Cato remained Caesar's major conservative nemesis. Taken aback by the Senate's reaction, Caesar wrote a letter from Gaul insisting that he had attacked the Usipetes and the Tencteri not for the sheer love of killing but to set an example that, he claimed, would deter further unrest among tribes subjected by Rome.

I, Gaius Caesar, would have been condemned in spite of all my achievements if I had not sought help from my armies.
—JULIUS CAESAR

Meanwhile, even before news of the massacre had reached Rome, Caesar had begun a new campaign. He sought to go where no Roman had ever been before: the other side of the Rhine River. His official explanation for the foray was the dubious claim that some of the Usipete and Tencteri cavalry had escaped over the Rhine during the massacre. The real aim of the mission, however, was almost purely symbolic: to establish a temporary stronghold on the far side of the river to demonstrate to German tribes that Roman interests extended beyond the Rhine. Caesar ordered his engineers to construct a bridge; within 10 days they had completed a massive wooden trestle bridge 1,500 feet long and 40 feet wide — a remarkable engineering achievement. Caesar's men crossed the bridge legion by legion, marching as if in a parade. After 18 days on the far side of the river, unchallenged by a single German band, Caesar led his troops back into Gaul, satisfied that he had made his point.

6

Britain and Other Challenges

> ***To argue that we ought not to go to war is only to say that we ought not to be rich, that we ought not to rule over others, that we ought neither to be free nor to be Romans.***
>
> —JULIUS CAESAR
> in his book
> *The Gallic Wars*

News of Caesar's penetration of unexplored lands on the far side of the Rhine generated great excitement in Rome. Later in 55 B.C., he set out on another adventure that further stirred the popular imagination. His destination this time was Britain, which to Romans was a mysterious, exotic land located somewhere near the edge of the world. Their only knowledge of the island had been acquired secondhand, from Gallic sailors who carried on sea trade with its inhabitants. Hearing of its strange white cliffs, they suspected that it was a cornucopia of riches. Caesar himself was enchanted by rumors of gold, silver, tin, and pearls. He also knew that if he could establish a port in Britain, replete with garrisons and warehouses, he could greatly increase Rome's sea power and win tremendous glory for himself.

Transported by 80 galleys, Caesar's army left Gaul in July 55 B.C. In a hurry to begin the mission, so as to avoid being caught in Britain during the winter, they had to leave the cavalry behind. This did not faze Caesar, who, with customary optimism, expected his formidable legions to subdue the reportedly backward British population with relative ease.

An imaginative view of Caesar on his daring first expedition to Britain in 55 B.C. Like most Romans, Caesar thought that the island of Britain was located in a vast, wild ocean that encircled the known world.

THE BETTMANN ARCHIVE

THE BETTMANN ARCHIVE

Caesar (standing in the bow of his ship) and his men met fierce resistance upon landing in Britain. Unfavorable weather and persistent guerrilla attacks by the Britons forced Caesar to return to Gaul after only 18 days.

After crossing the British Channel, Caesar's legions arrived at Dover, where they saw a menacing crowd of tribal warriors gathered along the cliffs. Caesar decided not to attempt to land on the Dover beaches, where the Romans would be easy targets for the Britons' javelins, but to sail farther down the British coast to look for a safer landing area. At a harbor where resistance seemed minimal, the Roman galleys dropped anchor. The troops waded ashore in their full battle gear, protected by a hail of arrows from the Roman archers. Forming their traditional well-ordered lines, they were easily able to drive scattered bands of Britons back into the dense coastal forests. The siege of Britain appeared to be going as planned.

In the following days, however, after the Romans set up fortifications along the coast, they were victimized by an early form of guerrilla warfare. Driving swift two-wheeled war chariots, the Britons conducted deft hit-and-run attacks against the Roman camps. Materializing suddenly from the forest in these vehicles, they would charge at the Roman soldiers, hurl their spears, and then disappear again. Roman soldiers who wandered too far into the brush in search of food or fuel became easy victims for

British spear throwers. Without their cavalry, the Romans had difficulty combating the deadly harrassment. The weather posed an additional problem. Caesar's anchored fleet was severely damaged when fierce winds and high tides swept the area. Some of Caesar's men interpreted the storms as bad omens foretelling ill fortune in the campaigns that lay ahead. The campaign was hopelessly bogged down. Enraged and embarrassed, Caesar decided, after only 18 days in Britain, to return to Gaul to regroup.

Cowards die many times before their deaths; the valiant never taste of death but once.
—JULIUS CAESAR
in Shakespeare's
Julius Caesar

Caesar realized that he would need to invade with far greater force in order to subject the tribes of Britain to Roman rule. Over the winter, he oversaw the construction of additional boats, specifically designed for British conditions. The vessels were built with especially low decks to facilitate landing on the beach. To take advantage of strong channel winds, they each carried sails and sophisticated rigging in addition to oars. Transports for carrying the cavalry's horses were given particularly broad hulls. In late spring 54 B.C., Caesar and his army of 4,000 men embarked for Britain. They sailed in a huge flotilla of 600 transports, 28 warships, and 200 private ships donated by Roman businessmen.

After landing on the British coast, near what is now the city of Sandwich, Caesar's army prepared for an inland expedition. They were guided through the unfamiliar twists and turns of the British forest by a collaborating tribesman named Mandubracius. Setting out at midnight, the Romans marched at a furious pace to Sturry, catching the few British bands they encountered on the way completely by surprise; most of the native armies, which were united under the leadership of Cassivellaunus, had withdrawn to an area northwest of present-day London. After a day, however, the expedition was stalled by news that several of the Roman ships anchored off the coast in an unprotected harbor had fallen prey to the unforgiving British weather. By messenger, Caesar directed the soldiers guarding the fleet to haul the rest of the ships on to the beach and build shelters for them. He also requested Labienus, his second-in-command in Gaul, to send over new

Fear nothing; you carry Caesar and his fortune.

—JULIUS CAESAR
to his ship's pilot on the way to Britain, 55 B.C.

vessels to replace the 40 ruined ones. Continuing onward, the Romans were subjected to an increasing number of guerrilla attacks. Nevertheless, they managed to cross the River Thames.

On the far side of the Thames, the Romans caught up with Cassivellaunus, whose troops were dug in around his capital city, Wheathampstead, near the site of modern St. Albans. In the climactic battle of the campaign, the Romans overwhelmed Cassivellaunus and captured his capital. The Briton leader agreed to surrender and to give up several "hostages" for Caesar to pack off to Rome as evidence of his military success. Even though this was a tremendous victory, Caesar had already recognized that his desire to make Britain a Roman province was unrealistic. A permanent military occupation would have to be imposed in order to control the island. There were not sufficient troops for this; in addition, there were barely enough supplies for even a few Roman troops to survive the harsh British winter. In September 54 B.C., after three months in Britain, Caesar returned home. It would be a hundred years before any part of the island would join the Roman Empire.

Though Caesar's conquest of Britain had been only temporary, it made impressive propaganda with which to promote his military reputation. A master of self-promotion, Caesar sent home exaggerated tales of brilliant campaigns against exotic peoples. Thus, the real battle had been won, for in the British adventure, as in the rest of his campaigns, Caesar considered military prestige to be far more important than actual conquests.

While Caesar was in Britain, the political situation at home had taken a turn for the worse. Though officially designated the governor of Spain, Pompey had remained in Rome and had been asked by a prominent politician named Hirrus to become dictator. Though Pompey declined the offer and appeared to have withdrawn for the most part from the continuing struggle between optimates and populares, it was widely rumored that he hoped through inactivity to destabilize the Republic and hence to create conditions in which he himself could seize control.

In August 54 B.C., Julia, Caesar's daughter and Pompey's wife, had died in childbirth. Doctors had traced her death to an event two years earlier, when, upon seeing a cloak of her husband's bloodied by violent senatorial debate, she had fainted and had a miscarriage. For Caesar, Julia's loss was both a personal and political tragedy. Julia had been his most important link to Pompey. Her death came at a time when Pompey was being courted by many members of the conservative bloc, who saw him as a lesser evil than Caesar. If Pompey were coopted by the optimates, the triumvirate would soon come to an end.

Meanwhile, Caesar's hold on Gaul was threatened. During his first years in Gaul, Caesar had pacified much of the region by winning brilliant military victories, securing a broad network of alliances, and installing a full-time military occupation. Upon returning from Britain in the fall of 54 B.C., Caesar found several revolts in progress. He learned that one of his garrisons in northeastern Gaul had been overwhelmed by the Eburones, a Belgic tribe led by Ambiorix. All 1,500 Roman troops manning the garrison had been slaughtered. Before slaying the Roman commander with a javelin, Ambiorix had completely humiliated him, ripping off his clothes and demanding, "How can creatures like you hope to rule over great men like us?" At the same time, the Nervii, who had barely escaped annihilation by Caesar in 57 B.C., were laying siege to a Roman garrison commanded by Marcus Cicero's brother, Quintus. Arriving in Gaul just in time to save Quintus's men, Caesar was shocked at the sophistication of the Belgian siege equipment. A third revolt, by the northeastern Treveri, was put down by Titus Labienus, the commander of the cavalry.

To prevent further revolts, Caesar decided to forgo his customary trip south to Cisalpine Gaul for the winter. He vowed that he would not cut his hair or shave his beard until Gaul was again under his control. Holding a conference at Amiens in early 53 B.C., Caesar managed to win some of the Gallic tribes back into the fold with promises of money and Roman protection against larger groups. Other tribes submitted after Caesar moved his main headquar-

THE BETTMANN ARCHIVE

Caesar accepts the surrender of Cassivellaunus and other British leaders during his second expedition to Britain in 54 B.C. Caesar's conquest of Britain proved to be only temporary, as he could not afford to maintain a permanent military presence there.

Since Gaul eventually became medieval France, the heartland of Western culture in the Middle Ages, it might truthfully be said that Caesar's conquest of Gaul was his most important contribution to history.

—CHESTER G. STARR
modern historian

ters to Lutetia, closer to their strongholds. It was then time to return to the far side of the Rhine. There, with the help of local collaborators, he killed off most of the Eburones. The notorious Ambiorix, however, managed to escape. Caesar had hoped to execute Ambiorix publicly as a warning to other rebellious tribes.

Feeling that some sort of symbolic act of revenge was necessary, Caesar instead decided to kill a less important rebel chief, Acco of the Senones. Before a conference of Gallic princes, Acco was executed in the brutal Roman manner. After all of his clothes were removed, his head was tied to a wooden fork; then he was beaten to death with rods and decapitated. By the autumn of 53 B.C., Caesar appeared to have eliminated all the rebels, but the spirit of rebellion continued to simmer. Ambiorix's annihilation of the Roman garrison had profoundly affected Gallic tribal leaders. In private, they now wondered whether it would be possible to drive Caesar away; perhaps, they imagined, Caesar was not invincible after all.

Caesar spent the winter of 53–52 B.C. in Cisalpine Gaul monitoring political developments in Rome. He was not pleased with what he observed. The alignment of forces had changed dramatically. Earlier that year, Crassus, as governor of Asia, had begun a military campaign against Parthia, an empire located in the territory that today makes up Iran. Crassus had hoped that by conquering Parthia he could keep in step with his powerful fellow triumvirs, both of whose reputations had been markedly enhanced by celebrated military exploits. But in June he and three-quarters of his men were killed in the worst defeat Rome had suffered in 150 years. The Parthians had surprised Crassus's men with an unusual military tactic. Riding on camels, the Asian archers fired a steady stream of arrows at two different trajectories, rendering Roman shields useless. It was said that Crassus's head had been delivered to the Parthian king on a platter. The king ordered molten gold to be poured into the rich man's mouth, saying, "Here, you have been greedy for this all your life. Eat it now."

Crassus had held the triumvirate together, serving as a mediator between Pompey and Caesar, with their huge egos and their grandiose schemes. With his death, the alliance dissolved almost completely. As the year 52 B.C. began, political turmoil left Rome without consuls. Conservatives, who usually opposed the subversion of republican institutions of government, promoted the idea of a dictatorship led by Pompey. In the words of historian Michael Grant, they wanted Pompey to give "a masterful turn to the helm and enable the old constitution to forge ahead." Eventually, the optimates engineered the election of Pompey to the open consulship, which, along with his governorship of Spain, made him extremely powerful.

So soon did so vast an army dissolve and vanish like a ghost or dream.
—PLUTARCH
Greek historian on Caesar's defeat of Vercingetorix

Caesar attempted to mend his relationship with Pompey by officially endorsing his consulship and by proposing a new marital arrangement. He offered to divorce his wife, Calpurnia, in order to marry Pompey's daughter and suggested that Pompey in turn marry Caesar's grandniece, Octavia. Pompey declined the offer and instead married the daughter of a corrupt conservative, Metellus Scipio, whom, later in the year, he would designate as a co-consul. It was a significant gesture. Pompey, clearly threatened by and jealous of Caesar's new wealth and prestige, had moved far away from his rival — though he had not forged a complete break. The conservatives now seemed willing to throw their full weight behind Pompey—at least until Caesar was eliminated.

For Caesar, these political concerns in Rome would have to wait, for in the winter of 52 B.C. the tribes of Gaul once again rebelled against Roman rule. Where the disunity of the Gallic tribes had facilitated Caesar's early success, their common hatred of Caesar and the Roman legions had finally united the disparate tribes. Now, together, they prayed to their war god, the wild boar, for deliverance from the Roman devils who had destroyed their land and killed their people. Although most of their soldiers were untrained peasants, they had a magnificent cavalry — wealthy horsemen wearing helmets covered with precious gems. Most importantly, they now had a strong leader, Vercingetorix, a brash

Under the leadership of Vercingetorix, the Gallic tribes rebelled against Roman rule in 52 B.C. After being defeated by Caesar in the siege of Alesia, Vercingetorix (on horseback) laid down his weapons and surrendered to the Roman conqueror.

and confident young nobleman who had accomplished the seemingly impossible task of uniting the many Gallic tribes into a massive army.

Determined to crush the newest Gallic rebellion, Caesar mounted an offensive in the spring of 52 B.C. He laid siege to Vercingetorix and a force estimated at 80,000 warriors at the fortified city of Alesia (just north of Dijon). One hundred thousand reinforcements came to the aid of the surrounded Gauls but were badly defeated by the Roman legions. An attempted night breakout resulted in heavy losses for Vercingetorix's men. When a third attempt to relieve the siege was defeated, Vercingetorix surrendered, laying his weapons at Caesar's feet. The siege had lasted less than one month. The Gallic leader was led back to Rome in chains, to be paraded as proof of Caesar's success in Gaul.

Even though Caesar would face another year of minor skirmishes, the victory at Alesia had assured his full triumph in the Gallic Wars. By the end of 51 B.C., after a decade of fighting, Julius Caesar was master of Gaul. It had been an unprecedented triumph. Caesar, in the name of Rome, had successfully laid claim to an area that stretched over 200,000 square miles. In more than 30 campaigns he had captured hundreds of towns, killed hundreds of thousands of men, women, and children. The slave markets of Rome were now glutted with men he had captured and sold. Through his conquests, Caesar had brought Mediterranean civilization and northern Europe into close contact, thereby transforming both the Roman Empire and the Gallic world. It was an immense achievement.

The defeat of Vercingetorix completed Caesar's conquest of Gaul. The Gallic campaigns brought tremendous riches to Rome and supplied thousands of slaves to markets like the one pictured here.

IVLIVS

7

The Die Is Cast

> ***When the swords flash, let no idea of love, piety, or even the face of your fathers move you. If they oppose you, let the blood of your own fathers flow from your blade.***
> —JULIUS CAESAR

Caesar's return to politics promised to be difficult. Once he gave up his military command, he would surely lose the immunity that his position conferred. He would then inevitably face prosecutions — for bribery and using force in politics — from conservatives hoping to drive him into exile. To avoid being tried in the Roman courts, he would have to secure a political office whose term overlapped with the end of his governorship in Gaul.

He decided to seek the consulship of 48 B.C. the election for which would be held in 49 B.C. He anticipated no problem in retaining his command until then; the major obstacle to his plan was the requirement that a candidate be a private citizen living in Rome. With the support of his many allies in Rome, Caesar won passage of a bill allowing him to run for the consulship *in absentia*. At first, Pompey agreed to support the law but soon thereafter changed his mind and joined conservatives who refused to recognize it. Caesar's future remained uncertain. Although his tremendous wealth had enabled him to purchase the support of much of Rome, he had broken completely with Pompey.

In 51 B.C., as Caesar waited anxiously with his army in Cisalpine Gaul, the conservative bloc in the Senate attempted to rally support for his immediate removal from Gaul. They were led by the consul Mar-

A 16th-century Limoges platter portrays a bearded Caesar on horseback. By 51 B.C., when Caesar began preparing to return to politics, the triumvirate had been shattered by Crassus's death and Pompey's desertion to the optimate camp.

ART RESOURCE

> ***Do you see what a man [Caesar] the Republic is up against, his foresight, his alertness, his readiness.***
> —MARCUS CICERO

cus Marcellus, who also flouted Caesar's provincial authority by conspicuously violating one of his regional laws. Though Caesar had granted the inhabitants of Cisalpine Gaul full Roman citizenship — which entitled them to immunity from flogging — Marcellus inflicted such punishment on one of Caesar's subjects in a public arena in Rome. Despite the apparent ascendancy of the conservatives, Caesar continued to influence Roman affairs through the consul for 50 B.C., Lucius Aemilius — whose support he had won with a bribe equivalent to $2,500,000 — and through the tribune Gaius Scribonius Curio.

From March to May of the year 50 B.C. vicious debates raged in the Senate over whether to install a successor to Caesar in Gaul. Curio effectively vetoed all attempts to pass such a law, gradually forcing a complete stalemate. The operation of the government lurched to a halt. Finally, Curio proposed a clever compromise, suggesting that Caesar give up his military command on the condition that he be allowed to stand for the election of 49 B.C. and that Pompey forfeit his own military command. The proposal had great appeal to the majority of Roman politicians, who feared that the burgeoning conflict between Caesar and Pompey might soon plunge the country into civil war, but a small group of diehard senators managed to block passage of the bill.

They also pushed through a measure requiring Caesar to surrender two of his legions. Seeking to quiet suspicions about his intentions, Caesar assented to the demand and as a gesture of good faith kept most of the rest of his army stationed on the northern side of the Alps. At the end of 50 B.C., Curio's compromise was again discussed by the Senate, and on December 1 it was approved by a huge majority — 370 to 22. The conservatives again managed to obtain a veto. That a measure with such widespread support could not win approval was an indication of the extent to which democratic institutions had decayed. At the same time, the lopsided endorsement of a bill that seemed to favor Caesar suggested to many conservatives, including Gaius Marcellus, consul for 50 B.C., that most Romans would be willing to give in to Caesar. Quick action was needed. Going to Pompey's quarters outside of Rome, Marcellus placed a sword in the general's hands and asked him to take whatever steps were necessary to protect the state. Pompey agreed to accept the position "unless a better way can be found." He also agreed to begin mounting an army.

In December negotiations were held between representatives of Caesar and Pompey at the behest of Senate members who were alarmed by Pompey's mobilization. Caesar's agents included Marcus Antonius, or Marc Antony (as he is known to history as a result of his appellation in Shakespeare's *Julius Caesar* and *Antony and Cleopatra*), who had replaced Curio as a tribune on December 10. Caesar made various proposals, even suggesting at one point that he would be satisfied with the allotment of a single legion and the governorship of the relatively insignificant province of Illyricum. Pompey would not yield. Even as the governor of Illyricum, Pompey reasoned, Caesar would pose a threat. On January 1, 49 B.C., at a Senate meeting, Antony tried to read a letter from Caesar reiterating his refusal to give up his command unless Pompey followed suit. He was shouted down, and the Senate proceeded to pass a measure demanding that Caesar relinquish his command by a certain date or be declared an outlaw. On January 7 the Senate officially validated Pompey's de facto dictatorship and instituted martial law.

Antony was forced to flee. Abandoning negotiations, Caesar prepared for a military invasion of Rome. On January 10, 49 B.C., he led a single legion over a small stream called the Rubicon, which separated Cisalpine Gaul from eastern Italy. In so doing, he committed treason, violating Sulla's law prohibiting a provincial governor from commanding troops outside his dominion. Caesar realized he was taking an irreversible step. As his troops marched into Italy, he uttered the immortal phrase "The die is cast." (The occasion would eventually give rise to an expression commonly used in many languages—"crossing the Rubicon"—which means taking final or decisive action.) Thus began a con-

ALINARI/ART RESOURCE

After being elected tribune in December 50 B.C., Marc Antony served as Caesar's envoy in Rome. In debates on the Senate floor, Antony fought attempts by Pompey and his conservative allies to strip Caesar of his command in Gaul.

Caesar crosses the Rubicon in 49 B.C., launching a military invasion of Rome and initiating the Roman Civil War. He had finally given up on negotiations aimed at ending his dispute with Pompey.

flict known to history as the Roman Civil War.

Caesar's invasion was an extremely risky venture. Pompey not only had the support of all the senior senators, but as the official leader of Rome, he also had access to local government troops and many provincial armies. Before Pompey had time to react, Caesar moved rapidly down the eastern coast of Italy, occupying several towns. In most of the regions that he traveled through, he was given a hearty welcome. Several garrisons that were expected to challenge his advance supported it instead. The conservatives were shocked, having completely underestimated the number of Romans who considered Caesar the legitimate heir to power.

After his initial victories, Caesar tried to persuade Pompey to meet with him to forge a compromise settlement, but Pompey ignored several requests by Caesar to negotiate. The optimates were disheartened to learn that although Pompey had agreed to defend Rome, he actually had at his disposal only the two legions Caesar had earlier surrendered. Obviously, these would be no match for Caesar's battle-hardened veterans of the Gallic Wars, and their loyalty was also suspect. Accompanied by the conservative senators and the two consuls, Pompey abandoned Rome and fled southward, intending to escape to Greece, where he hoped to assemble a larger army and ultimately join with the forces nominally still under his command in Spain. He departed for Greece in March 49 B.C. from the port of Brundisium (Brindisi), being forced to execute several deft naval maneuvers to avoid capture.

Caesar could not pursue Pompey until transports and warships were built to ferry his army across the Adriatic Sea. In the meantime, he returned to the outskirts of Rome, where he set up camp, hoping to raise money. Even the tremendous riches Caesar had accumulated in Gaul were not enough to bankroll a campaign against Pompey and the Roman government. He also hoped to establish control over the leaderless government and to recruit senators who remained undecided. Convening the Roman assembly outside the city, he won the support of most members with offers of future monetary favors. A meeting with Senate members, convened on April 1, 49 B.C., was less successful, as few powerful nobles appeared. Irritated by this lukewarm reaction, Caesar declared, "I earnestly invite you to join with me in carrying on the government of Rome. If, however, timidity makes you shrink from the task, I shall trouble you no more. For in that case I shall govern myself." Nevertheless, the Senate later endorsed Caesar's plan to withdraw funds from the reserve treasury, which had been left behind by Pompey and his followers in their hurried exit. Caesar's access to the treasury was then blocked by the tribune Caecilius Metellus, so he had to enter the city — violating the prohibition against incumbent governors entering Rome — and threaten to kill the tribune. These actions were extremely unpopular, and as Caesar prepared to leave Rome to combat Pompey, he was no longer sure of the continued support of the populace.

To preclude any further loss of popularity, Caesar took steps to assure the flow of grain to Rome. Most of the city's supply was imported by sea from the provinces and was susceptible to interdiction by Pompey's powerful naval forces. At Caesar's behest, Curio seized the islands of Sicily and Sardinia and confiscated the islands' rich stores of corn and wheat.

Caesar's strategy was to go first to Spain, to defeat

Caesar had never hated Pompey. They were both men of great charm, and their purely personal relations had often been warm. Ultimately, however, it had simply been impossible for both of them to occupy the same political position at Rome that each craved.

—FRITZ M. HEICHELHEIM
modern historian

I dread this terrible war, the like of which has never been seen.

—MARCUS CICERO
at the beginning of the
Roman Civil War in 49 B.C.

Pompey's now leaderless legions there, and then to return to Italy and cross to Greece, where Pompey was gathering an army. "I am going to Spain to fight an army without a general," he said, "and then to the east to fight a general without an army." On his way, he passed through Massilia (Marseilles), a city-state on the Mediterranean that appeared to be friendly. After his departure, however, the city invited optimate leader Ahenobarbus to lead its defenses and cut off Caesar's communication routes back to Rome. After dispatching part of his army to return to Massilia, Caesar traveled on to Spain, where, on June 22, he met up with six of his legions that had been stationed in Gaul.

Worried about having left Italy unguarded and about the situation in Massilia, Caesar quickly sought out Pompey's legions. In his haste, he almost led his army to disaster. After they crossed a bridge onto a peninsula, the bridge was washed away, and they were stranded between two large rivers, both of which were swollen with melted snow. They were only able to escape by constructing makeshift bridges they had learned about in Britain.

Aided by allies he had made during earlier tours of duty in Spain, Caesar caught up to and surrounded the Pompeian army at Ilerda. Instead of attacking, he laid siege to the enemy camp and, after 40 days during which very little blood was spilled, starved the Pompeians into submission. Caesar was the magnanimous conqueror, offering captured soldiers the chance to join his legions, sending others back to their homes. The defeated army in Spain, after all, was made up not of Gauls but of Romans. These were people whom Caesar intended to rule, not crush. On his return, Caesar discovered that his forces had defeated Ahenobarbus in Massilia. Through extending clemency to Massilia's people, Caesar subordinated the city to Rome, ending its long history of independent statehood.

As Caesar's army marched through Placentia on its way back to Rome, a major mutiny broke out. It was the first time during Caesar's long military career that his troops had revolted. The soldiers had several complaints: their units had suffered severe losses in the initial skirmishes in Spain, they had not been fed well during the lengthy siege of Ilerda, and they were upset by Caesar's policy of clemency because it often left them with much smaller amounts of loot. After subduing the uprising, Caesar announced his intention to impose severe penalties on the offending legions in order to discourage future mutinies. He threatened to kill every tenth man — the traditional Roman punishment for mutinies. But he later agreed to execute a total of only 12 soldiers.

Caesar returned to Rome to establish some semblance of orderly government. Spending only 11 days in the capital, he accomplished much. First of all, he had himself temporarily appointed dictator. He did so primarily in order to acquire the constitutional power to arrange for consular elections — not in order to institute repressive measures, as Sulla had done. He also used the position to address the question of financial reform. Personal debt had become an enormous problem for the Roman economy. The crisis of the Civil War threatened to force into bankruptcy many rich creditors whose clients had no way of paying back massive debts. Caesar passed bills making it easier for debtors to meet their obligations. The measures forced creditors to accept land and material possessions as payment in lieu of money and allowed debtors to deduct interest costs. The law scared many of Caesar's richer supporters, who worried that he might eventually declare all debts to be invalid. To accommodate the Marian nobles, Caesar restored civil rights to those who had lost them during Sulla's reign. He also allowed many political exiles to return.

Finally, Caesar organized elections. With Pompey's political followers either out of the country or silenced, there was little doubt of the outcome. Caesar was elected consul for 48 B.C. and soon installed his friends in all the most important positions. Now it was Caesar, not Pompey, who commanded the governmental power of Rome. It was Pompey, not Caesar, who was the outlaw.

As winter approached, many Romans wondered whether Pompey might soon attempt to return to

THE BETTMANN ARCHIVE

Having forced Pompey to retreat to Greece and having defeated Pompeian troops in Spain, Caesar triumphantly enters Rome in 49 B.C. On a whirlwind 11-day visit, Caesar had himself appointed dictator and carried out extensive financial reforms.

SEF/ART RESOURCE

In January 48 B.C., Caesar led an armada across the Adriatic Sea in pursuit of Pompey. Nine months later, he defeated Pompey's army decisively at the Battle of Pharsalus, depicted here in a 15th-century Swiss tapestry.

Italy. Preferring not to wait for his enemy's next move, Caesar set sail for Greece from Brundisium on January 4, 48 B.C. Fewer transports were available than expected, forcing him to leave many of his men behind. In Greece, Pompey was relaxing in Thessalonica, not expecting Caesar to venture across the Adriatic until spring brought better weather. Skillfully eluding Pompey's 100-vessel navy, led by Bibulus, Caesar landed on the coast of what is now Albania.

His camp was soon visited by several men claiming to be deserters from Pompey's army. They were betraying Pompey, they said, and had valuable information for Caesar. Based on the story supplied by the agents, Caesar led a detachment of soldiers toward the city of Dyrrhachium (Durres). Caesar had fallen for a ploy. His forces were ambushed and almost trapped, and Caesar was lucky to survive.

On August 9, after several months of shifting positions and scrambling for advantage, the two armies faced each other at Pharsalus, which lay in open area known as the Thessalian Plain. Far from being a general without an army, Pompey commanded forces that outnumbered Caesar's by more than two to one. It made little difference. Caesar's troops, having fought for years together in Gaul, were a tightly knit, well-trained group. Pompey's troops could not match their instinctive ability to work together and fell back before the savage charge of Caesar's legions. The battle was soon a rout. Most of Pompey's men were finally trapped by Caesar's legions on a plateau overlooking a river. Unable to descend the heights, pinned by Caesar's relentless pressure, they surrendered. Many thousands of lives were lost at Pharsalus, the overwhelming number of them from Pompey's forces. It had been the largest battle ever fought between Romans.

Before the battle, Caesar had given his officers a list of the men in Pompey's ranks who should be spared. Among them was Marcus Brutus, the son of one of Caesar's lovers and a man who some historians thought was actually Caesar's son. Pompey himself managed to escape.

THE BETTMANN ARCHIVE

Marcus Brutus was a scholarly, serious, and idealistic Roman statesman. The son of Caesar's favorite mistress, Brutus was one of many members of Pompey's army pardoned by the victorious dictator after the Battle of Pharsalus.

Bonfils
7

8

Egyptian Intrigue

He was spellbound the moment he set eyes on her and she opened her mouth to speak.
—DIO CASSIUS
Roman historian, on Caesar's infatuation with Cleopatra

Now truly a general without an army, Pompey fled for his life. With a few advisers he sailed to Egypt, hoping that since he had supported Egypt's boy-king Ptolemy XIII in his battle with his sister Cleopatra for the Egyptian throne, he might find refuge there. But as Pompey's boat dropped anchor off the coast near the Egyptian capital of Alexandria on September 28, 48 B.C., Egypt's dynastic quarrel threatened to bounce Ptolemy XIII from the throne. His sister Cleopatra, who had been forced to yield her half of the throne a year earlier by Ptolemy's three advisers, was preparing to attack the government's forces at Pelesium. Pompey sent a request for asylum to Ptolemy's aides, Achilles, Pothinus, and Theodotus, who, as the ruling council, exercised real control over the Egyptian state.

The council had a difficult decision to make. If they accepted Pompey, they would run the risk of incurring Caesar's enmity. If they turned Pompey away, however, he was certain to ally himself with Cleopatra. Theodotus convinced his compatriots that the only choice was to put Pompey to death. Achilles was sent in a small boat to Pompey's ship to pretend to welcome him to Egypt. When Pompey set foot on Egyptian soil, he was struck down and assassinated.

Hot in pursuit of Pompey, Caesar arrived in Al-

An Egyptian relief portrays Cleopatra as the goddess Isis, the eternal mother of the Nile. Intelligent, beautiful, and ambitious, Cleopatra was nevertheless forced from the Egyptian throne by her brother Ptolemy XIII in 50 B.C., one year before Caesar landed in her country.

THE BETTMANN ARCHIVE

exandria a few days later and was presented with Pompey's head and signet ring. Supposedly, he wept at the sight. He was glad to have Pompey out of the way but was sorry that his death had come at the hands of the Egyptians, whom he considered inferior to Romans. In addition to pursuing Pompey, Caesar had another reason for being in Alexandria: to attempt to exploit the fabulously wealthy country.

Alexandria in 48 B.C. was a spider's web of royal politics. If Rome had its share of political intrigue and plotting, Egypt fed on it. The prize was royalty; the combatants were a bizarre mixture of young pretenders to the throne, their scheming advisers, their bodyguards and military chieftains, their fortune-tellers and magicians, their servants and admirers.

Arriving in Alexandria, Egypt, in pursuit of Pompey, Caesar is presented with his rival's head. The Roman general had been murdered by Egypt's ruling council — advisors to the country's boy-king, Ptolemy XIII.

Egypt was an independent kingdom that had been ruled for many generations by a line of kings called the Ptolemies, descendants of a general who

THE BETTMANN ARCHIVE

THE BETTMANN ARCHIVE

> ***It was a tragic situation that the fate of Pompey the Great should have been determined by three such men [the Egyptian ruling council], and that he, riding at anchor off the shore, should have been forced to wait on the decision of such a tribunal.***
>
> —PLUTARCH
> Greek historian

Cleopatra presents herself to Caesar after being smuggled into his chambers in a rug. According to legend, Caesar fell immediately in love with her and quickly pledged to support her campaign for the Egyptian throne.

served under Alexander the Great. Three years before Caesar's arrival in Egypt, King Ptolemy XII, or Auletes, had died, leaving the throne to his daughter, Cleopatra VII, and his son, Ptolemy XIII. She was then 18 and he 10. As the father had willed, the two became co-rulers, a situation that quickly gave rise to conflict and rivalry. Scores of crafty henchmen insinuated themselves into the favor of Cleopatra and her brother. Anxious to acquire even greater influence, advisers for each sibling urged their leader to oust the other.

By the time Caesar arrived with a small, elite force of 1,200 men, Ptolemy XIII had done just that, driving Cleopatra into exile. But the ruling council was still uneasy, for Cleopatra was a clever and dangerous woman. As described by Greek historian Plutarch, she had "irresistible charm," a delightful manner, and a voice "like a lyre." Above all, she was

I will make all the men I love kings. I will make you a king. I will have many young kings with round strong arms; and when I am tired of them I will whip them to death; but you shall always be my king; my nice, kind, wise, good old king.

—CLEOPATRA
addressing Caesar in
George Bernard Shaw's
play *Caesar and Cleopatra*

willing to use her ability to attract men toward political ends.

In Alexandria, Caesar settled in the royal palace. His troops had entered the city in a triumphal procession headed by standard-bearers who carried aloft the *fasces*, an ax with a bundle of rods symbolizing Roman authority. This show of force had offended Egyptian citizens and prompted widespread riots. Caesar caused further discord by demanding that Egyptian leaders repay the debts incurred with Rome by Ptolemy XII. In turn, the ruling council treated Caesar with shocking rudeness. When Caesar ordered food for his troops, Pothinus sent moldy grain. When Caesar demanded food for himself, he was served on wooden dishes rather than the gold or silver plates customary for royal guests.

Meanwhile, Caesar took it upon himself to attempt arbitration of the Egyptian power struggle, claiming that a treaty he had signed with Ptolemy XII gave him the power to do so. He ordered Ptolemy XIII and Cleopatra to come before him. The ruling council agreed to the plan, thinking that their henchmen could easily intercept and do away with Cleopatra as she made her way into Alexandria. Cleopatra conceived a brilliant strategy by which to slip through her brother's men. She was transported into the city in a small boat, then had her attendant, a Sicilian named Apollodorus, wrap her up in "the cover of a bed" and carry her through the palace gates to Caesar's apartment. Once inside, she was unwrapped and introduced herself to the surprised but delighted Roman dictator.

The two were attracted to each other almost immediately. He saw in her the same kind of ambitious fire and gambling instincts that he saw in himself. She saw in him the world's most legendary figure, a man who could help her attain her rightful place as ruler of Egypt. The 52-year-old Caesar and the 21-year-old Cleopatra became lovers.

When young Ptolemy XIII discovered that his sister had entered the palace and was in the company of Caesar, he had a violent tantrum. Rumors soon began flying around Alexandria that the leader of the Romans was attempting to take over the kingdom of Egypt. A mob formed outside the palace walls. The Egyptian army stood ready to intervene. Although Caesar did not have a large military force at his side, he controlled the palace and its complex of buildings and, in effect, held two valuable hostages—Cleopatra and Ptolemy.

In the following weeks the Egyptian forces attacked the palace, only to be repulsed by Caesar's men. Caesar had earlier called for reinforcements, but until they arrived he had to hold out with his men inside the palace. The confrontation was later known as the Alexandrian War.

When a small number of Roman reinforcements landed by sea, Caesar temporarily left the palace, jumped aboard a small galley, and was almost killed. According to legend, he had to swim for safety, holding important dispatches in an upraised hand to keep them dry. He even lost his cloak, which was later displayed by Egyptians to mark their humiliation of Caesar.

After Caesar agreed to assist Cleopatra in the Egyptian dynastic struggle, Ptolemy XIII's forces trapped the Roman leader in the Egyptian palace. In an unsuccessful attempt to escape the siege, Caesar was forced to swim to safety, holding important documents above his head to keep them dry.

THE BETTMANN ARCHIVE

He often feasted with her until dawn; and they would have sailed together in her state barge nearly to Ethiopia had his soldiers consented to follow him.

—SUETONIUS
Roman historian,
describing Caesar's
relationship with Cleopatra

THE BETTMANN ARCHIVE

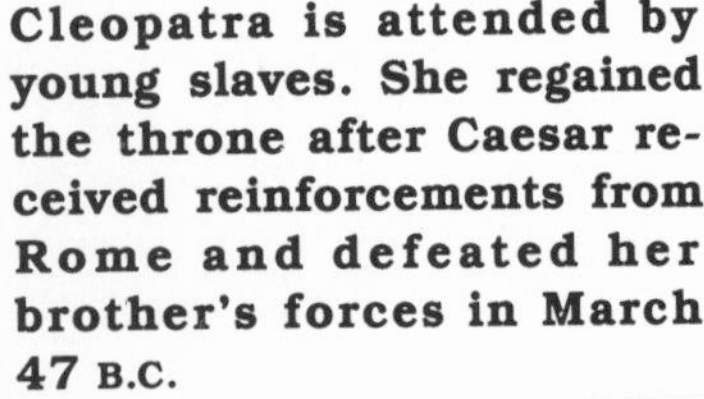

Cleopatra is attended by young slaves. She regained the throne after Caesar received reinforcements from Rome and defeated her brother's forces in March 47 B.C.

The Egyptian army's siege of the palace was finally broken in March 47 B.C., when Roman reinforcements finally arrived. Caesar then sent Ptolemy XIII from the palace to join the Egyptian army south of the Nile delta, where it was preparing for war. In releasing his prisoner, Caesar was not compromising with the enemy. He was in fact sentencing the boy-king to death. He knew that a major battle was imminent, one in which Ptolemy would be asked to lead the Egyptian forces, and he fully expected that the Roman army, now reinforced, would likely crush its enemy. It is said that Ptolemy cried when he left the palace. He, too, probably sensed that he was doomed.

The battle took place in early March 47 B.C. Much of the Egyptian army was annihilated. Ptolemy's body was identified by the gold royal armor that he wore. Cleopatra soon became the undisputed queen of Egypt.

After the final battle, Caesar stayed in Egypt for several more months. He now had time to appreciate Alexandria's gleaming white marble buildings, its magnificent works of art, its theater, public libraries, and schools — all the wonders of the city that for many years had made it the world's foremost center of culture and learning. His love of Alexandria would later inspire Caesar to promote a similar cultural explosion in Rome.

In the spring of 47 B.C., Caesar and Cleopatra embarked on a famous boat trip up the Nile River. Their vessel was accompanied by a large number of magnificent barges, and the Roman army paced along the riverbanks. The procession was unmatched in its gaudy display of riches and wealth.

Caesar and his lover Cleopatra sail triumphantly up the Nile River in a procession celebrating her return to power in the spring of 47 B.C. Their boat was made of precious woods and decorated with gold.

THE BETTMANN ARCHIVE

The cedar and cyprus royal boat was decorated in gold; special slaves rowed the boat gently through the water as the Egyptian people marveled at the splendor.

Caesar left Egypt and Cleopatra in June 47 B.C. A short time later Cleopatra gave birth to a son, Caesarion, or "Little Caesar," whom some historians think was Caesar's son.

In August 47 B.C., before returning to Rome, Caesar traveled to Pontus in Asia, where Pharnaces II, the son of Rome's old enemy Mithridates, was attempting to enlarge his kingdom by annexing lands under Roman control. The forces of Pharnaces and Caesar clashed in a five-day campaign at Zela, where Caesar devastated his opponent. In a dispatch to Rome, Caesar described his campaign with the famous words "I came, I saw, I conquered."

The conqueror returned to Rome in October 47 B.C. but only for a short time. A force of Caesar's enemies led by Cato, two of Pompey's sons, and Lab-

The Roman statesman Cato kills himself in order not to fall into Caesar's hands after the Pompeian army's defeat at Thapsus in 46 B.C.

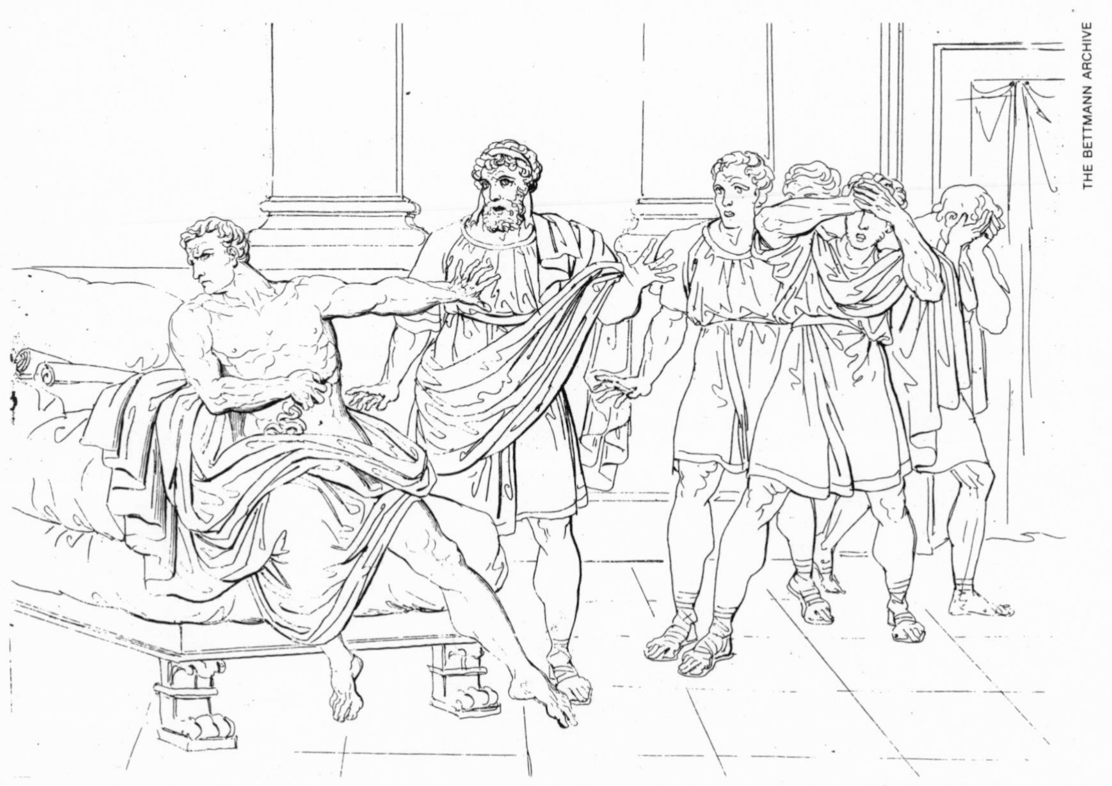

THE BETTMANN ARCHIVE

ienus, once one of Caesar's trusted generals, had assembled in North Africa to challenge Caesar's authority.

The first encounters in Africa were not very successful for Caesar. Many of his men were now relatively new and untrained recruits. Gradually, his energy, ingenuity, and resourcefulness prevailed. At the city of Thapsus, Caesar's army trapped a large contingent of the enemy and massacred them.

Caesar's victory at Thapsus ended the African resistance. Labienus and Pompey's sons fled to Spain, where they hoped to continue to fight. Cato, distraught over his military failure, at the prospect of a Rome run by Caesar, fell on his sword.

Caesar's short message to Rome after his defeat of Pharnaces — "Veni, Vidi, Vici" — served as a terse summation of his career to that point. In Gaul he had staked his claim as a superior military commander; he had carried the Roman standards to Britain and the untamed lands beyond the Rhine. At Pharsalus the defeat of Pompey established Caesar as the supreme political and military leader of the day; Thaspus assured his by then all but inevitable accession to ultimate power as the dictator of Rome. There were few worlds left for him to conquer.

It is doubtful whether Rome could at that time in any way compare with the grandeur and the sense of history and destiny that infused the very air of Alexandria.

—ERNLE BRADFORD
modern historian

VENI
VIDI
VICI
CLAVDIVS POPELIN INV ET PINXIT ENCAVSTO AN MDCCCLXIV

9

Master of Rome

> ***Danger knows full well that Caesar is more dangerous than he.***
>
> —JULIUS CAESAR
> in Shakespeare's
> *Julius Caesar*

The streets of Rome were covered with flowers. Altars throughout the city burned with incense. The massive crowd waited. Caesar was home, and Rome would now celebrate his heroic deeds.

Romans traditionally honored the victories of their military heroes with days of extravagant celebration called "triumphs." Now Julius Caesar was to receive an unprecedented number of triumphs — one each for his conquests of Gaul, Egypt, Africa, and Pharnaces in Asia Minor. These processions would be more spectacular than any the Roman people had ever witnessed.

The parade honoring the Gallic campaign featured a long line of wagons and chariots laden with statues, paintings, jewels, and other treasures taken in the wars. Romans were treated to a display of weapons, exotic religious objects, and great signs bearing the names of Caesar's victorious battles — strange and mysterious names to most Romans. Marching next to the floats were trumpeters, priests, musicians, and soldiers. Toward the end of the parade came Vercingetorix, in chains. The Gallic hero had been kept alive by Caesar for this day and only for this day. Following the parade he was executed. Then came an honor guard and city officials. Finally, there was Caesar, dressed in purple and gold, riding in his splendid triumphal chariot

In 45 B.C. Caesar returned permanently to Rome. After being named dictator for life, he enacted a broad slate of reforms. His arrogation of power and imperious manner led many to ask whether he had ambitions of becoming king.

THE BETTMANN ARCHIVE

A Renaissance woodcut portrays one of Caesar's four triumphs, honoring his victories in Gaul, Egypt, Africa, and Asia Minor. For ten days one lavish procession and spectacular event followed another in all parts of the city.

drawn by four horses. Later that day there were lavish banquets, theatrical performances, and public games.

For 10 days Rome was swept up by celebration as one extravagant event followed another. Four hundred lions were let loose in one of the stadiums, to be hunted by paying customers. There was a mock naval battle on an artificial lake built just for the occasion. For the triumph honoring the conquest of Egypt, Queen Cleopatra, with her son Caesarion, traveled to Rome. At a new forum Caesar built to honor his family clan, the dictator unveiled a golden statue of Cleopatra.

The huge numbers of people who had come to Rome from Italy and other provinces for the festivities slept in tents pitched on the streets. The press of humanity for some of the activities was so great that many Romans were crushed to death, incuding two senators. All of this was in honor of the man who had so relentlessly and brilliantly pursued power and won.

Caesar's hold on power was still not completely secure. He had to take to the field of battle one last time. The remnants of the Pompeian army had made a last desperate attack against the Roman forces in Spain. Hence, Caesar left Rome in November 46 B.C.

In March 45 B.C., outside the town of Munda in northern Spain, Caesar's army engaged the rebels, who were led by Pompey's sons and Labienus. The rebels fought fiercely at first, but finally their lines broke and Caesar's legions forced a surrender. Rome's bloody civil war was finally over.

Back in Rome, Caesar accepted powers greater than any Roman leader before him. He became dic-

Cleopatra and her retinue participate in one of Caesar's triumphs. Caesar placed an impressive statue honoring the Egyptian queen in Rome, causing many to wonder whether he would divorce Calpurnia and move the royal court to Alexandria.

THE BETTMANN ARCHIVE

THE BETTMANN ARCHIVE

In February 44 B.C. Caesar rejected Marc Antony's attempts to crown him king of Rome. Nevertheless, many Romans remained convinced that he sought to establish a monarchy.

tator for life. His every decree would now be accepted without question by the Senate or any other legal or legislative body. Statues of Caesar appeared everywhere; temples were dedicated in his honor. The month of Quintilis, the month of his birth, was renamed Julius. The republic, some Romans lamented, had come to an end.

Caesar had attained much on the battlefield through his bold, decisive leadership. Romans now were able to witness his administrative skills as he zealously plunged into the affairs of state. He reorganized the governmental structure of Italian towns, amended the criminal codes to impose more severe penalties for crimes of violence, and established a uniform system of customs dues to regulate monies coming into the treasury. He abolished the political clubs, the *collegia*, which had often been the source of violence during elections. He passed laws limiting the degree of luxury that might be displayed publicly, a direct slap at the aristocracy. He also started vast engineering projects, commissioning engineers to build roads across mountains and dig channels to control river flows. He planned for public libraries and theaters, in hopes that Rome would become a center for art and learning much like Alexandria. Caesar had carved out his own empire and had achieved power almost unparalleled in world history.

Yet, Caesar still provoked in many deep resentment and distrust. Was it ambition or patriotism that motivated his actions? Was he a tyrant or a hero? Caesar had killed thousands of men during his ascent to power. If he inspired some with his great accomplishments and promises of progress, he left others bitter with hatred, fearful of the future.

Was Rome soon to see a monarchy? Many Romans remained proud of their republican traditions and institutions. Although Caesar exercised dictatorial powers, this was perhaps necessary to restore order in a turbulent time. There had been other dictators, but ultimately Rome's traditional institutions had prevailed. A monarchy, with a hereditary succession, was a different matter indeed. Certainly Caesar was nearly playing the role of king already, dressing in luxurious clothes, surrounding himself with pomp and ceremony. If the people of Rome would accept him as a king, many believed, Caesar would seize the chance. His manner, his arrogance, his regal bearing all suggested this.

Although in front of a large crowd he three times removed a crown that Mark Antony placed on his head, and on another occasion told a cheering throng that he was Caesar, not *Rex* (king), his actions did not allay the suspicion and unrest surrounding him. It was said that he had renounced the republic as "a mere name without form or body." No one could be certain that he was sincere in appearing not to want the throne.

> ***When the murder [of Caesar] was newly done there were sudden outcries of people that ran up and down the city, the which indeed did the more increase the fear and tumult.***
> —PLUTARCH

THE BETTMANN ARCHIVE

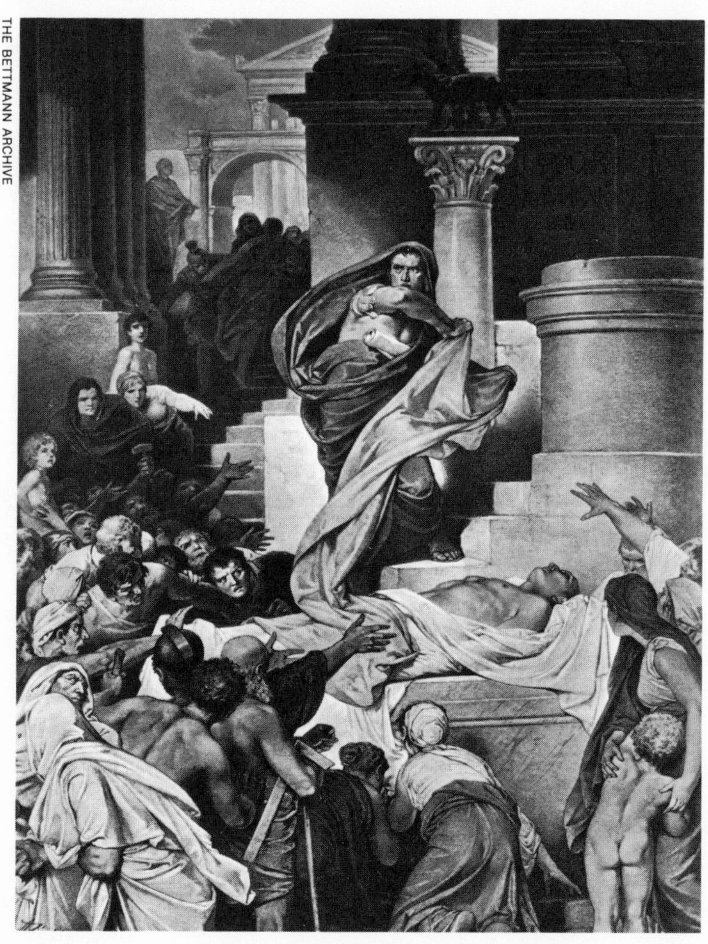

An 1883 illustration of Caesar's death scene from Shakespeare's *Julius Caesar*. The assassins believed his death would bring an end to dictatorship and restore the Roman republic.

CULVER PICTURES, INC.

As his murderers leave the Senate, waving their daggers in triumph, Caesar's body lies at the foot of a statue of Pompey. Instead of reviving the republic, his assassination led to fifteen years of civil war and to the ultimate establishment of the Roman Empire.

On many occasions during the Civil War, Caesar had dealt generously with his opponents. Such benevolence, he believed, had drawn former enemies to his side. Those pardoned had often learned to work with Caesar, even to admire him. Others, however, continued to perceive Caesar as leading Rome down a path of destruction. He had undermined the laws of the republic. No longer did Rome even pretend to be ruled by the representatives of the people. Many felt that Caesar must be stopped.

As March 44 B.C. approached, Caesar was all too aware of the enmity and mistrust he provoked. A series of omens foretold of great disturbances for Rome. Caesar was warned to be careful of his present safety. According to the Shakespeare play, he was told he should "beware the Ides of March."

The secret conspiracy to murder Caesar included at least 60 men. Its leaders were Gaius Cassius Longinus and his brother-in-law Marcus Junius Brutus. Both had fought against Caesar in the Civil War, and both owed their lives to his clemency. He had spared them and others in an attempt to stem the disunity that had plagued Rome for so many years.

> ***The abuse of greatness is when it disjoins remorse from power.***
> —BRUTUS
> in Shakespeare's
> *Julius Caesar*

Cassius was the ringleader of the plot. An able general under Pompey, he was now a minor office holder. Unlike Cassius, Brutus was actually a close friend of Caesar's — even though the two were political rivals. The dictator affectionately called Brutus "son." In view of Caesar's long love affair with Servilia, Brutus's mother, some wondered whether Caesar was actually Brutus's father. Brutus was scholarly, serious, and idealistic. He was often seen at the Forum and in the Senate delivering long orations. He greatly admired Cato, Caesar's rival, and he married Cato's daughter. Moreover, his family claimed an ancestral tradition of opposition to tyrants, tracing its heritage to Junius Brutus, who, according to legend, had overthrown and expelled the last Roman king, Tarquin the Proud.

To Brutus and Cassius and the others in the conspiracy, Julius Caesar was just such a tyrant and had to be stopped. They were driven by a mixture of idealism, personal jealousy, ambition, and desire for revenge. They feared that Caesar planned to establish himself as king, a step that might spell a permanent end to the republic.

Marc Antony delivers an impassioned funeral oration over Caesar's body. In Shakespeare's version, the speech begins with the famous lines, "Friends, Romans, countrymen, lend me your ears." Afterward, crowds rioted in the streets, vengefully attacking those who had allegedly supported Caesar's assassins.

CULVER PICTURES, INC.

Augustus Caesar, grandnephew of Julius, restored peace to Rome in 31 B.C. by establishing an empire. Six generations of Caesar's descendants succeeded him as *imperator*, or emperor of Rome.

A Roman coin bearing Caesar's profile. Although his historical impact was tremendous, historians' interpretations of his significance differ. Some see him as the founder of a new era, while others view him as the destroyer of the republic.

Ironically, Julius Caesar's reign ended at the base of a statue of Pompey. After receiving 23 dagger blows, Caesar died in a crumpled heap beneath Pompey's likeness. Afterward, the conspirators, waving their blood-stained weapons, ran through the streets of Rome proclaiming the return of liberty.

At the funeral, Mark Antony delivered an impassioned speech praising Caesar as a noble leader. Unfolding the bloody garments, cut through in many places, Antony worked the audience into a fury. They took Caesar's body, burned it ceremoniously in the market place, and sought out the assassins, crying "Kill the murderers." Brutus, Cassius, and the others were forced to flee the city. Liberty had not returned to Rome, as the conspirators had hoped it would. Instead, Caesar's murder ushered in a savage period of civil strife, a time of panic, confusion, reprisal, riot, and massacre. For over a decade the Romans, lacking strong leadership, suffered through one crisis after another as generals and politicians schemed and killed. Several thousand Romans, including Cicero, were executed. Both Brutus and Cassius committed suicide.

Not until Gaius Octavius, the grandnephew of Julius Caesar, seized power did Rome achieve relative peace and stability. Like Caesar he never assumed the title of king, but he ruled as a monarch with all power concentrated in his own person. He was the *imperator*, or "leader." He was called "Augustus," a name of reverence.

His granduncle Caesar had set the stage. He had thrown aside a republic that lacked decisive leadership, had secured for Rome vast new territories, and had laid the foundation for a vast empire.

It is said that the people of Rome saw a comet streaking across the sky for six nights following Caesar's death. Many believed it was his spirit flashing gloriously into the heavens, marking him as divine. On coins made after his death, he is pictured with a star above his head. A marble column in the Forum was inscribed with the words "To the Father of His Country."

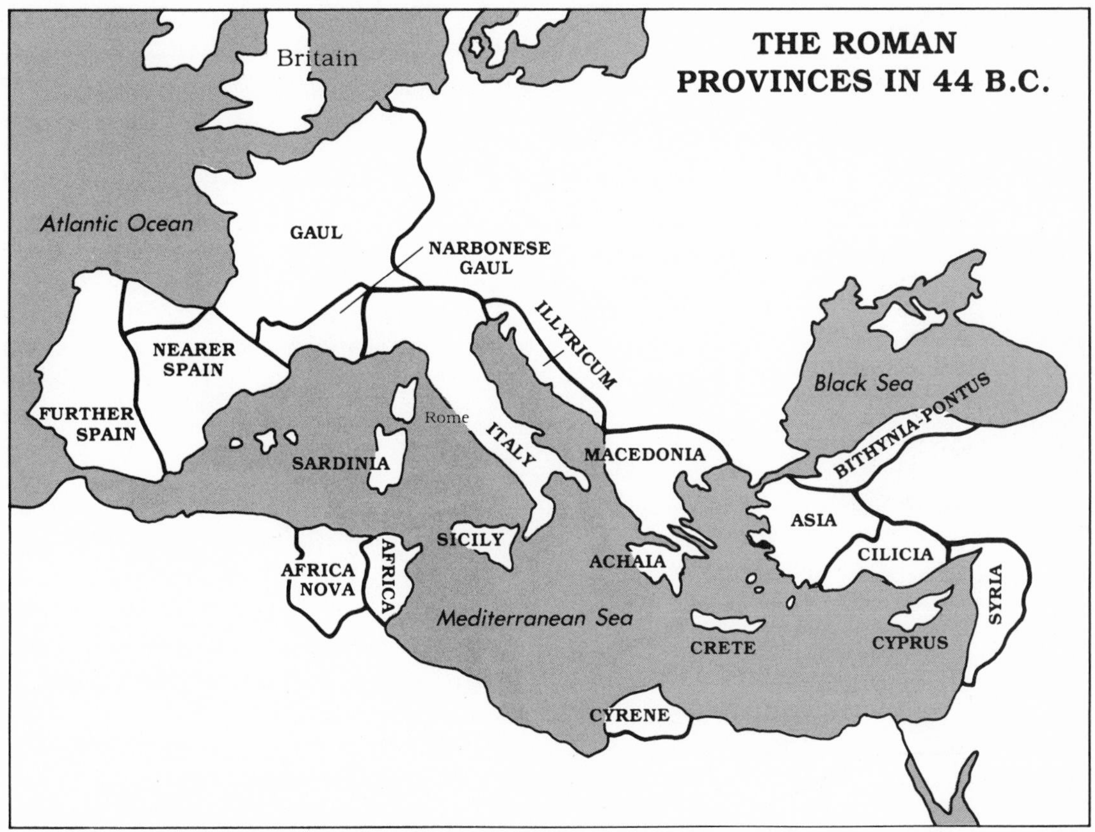

The people of Rome and historians of succeeding generations would disagree about his intentions, but all agreed on one point — that he had a tremendous impact on the history of Rome. Cicero, his enemy, said bitterly after Caesar's death, "We have killed the king, but the kingdom is still with us."

A map of Rome's domains at the time of Caesar's death in 44 B.C. In the succeeding 500 years, Roman emperors made further conquests, primarily in the Middle East and North Africa.

Further Reading

Asimov, Isaac. *The Roman Republic.* Boston: Houghton Mifflin, 1966.

Bradford, Ernle. *Julius Caesar: The Pursuit of Power.* New York: William Morrow, 1984.

Caesar, Gaius Julius. *War Commentaries*, ed. and trans. by John Warrington. New York: Dutton, 1958.

Carcopino, Jerome. *Daily Life in Ancient Rome.* New Haven: Yale University Press, 1958.

Ferrero, Guglielmo. *The Life of Caesar.* New York: W. W. Norton, 1962.

Grant, Michael. *Julius Caesar.* New York: McGraw-Hill, 1969.

———. *History of Rome.* New York: Scribners, 1978.

Isenberg, Irwin. *Caesar.* New York: American Heritage, 1964.

Kahn, Arthur. *The Education of Julius Caesar.* New York: Schocken, 1986.

Massie, Allan. *The Caesars.* New York: Franklin Watts, 1984.

Shakespeare, William. *Julius Caesar*, ed. by John Dover Wilson. Cambridge, England: Cambridge University Press, 1964.

Chronology

c. 100 B.C. Born Gaius Julius Caesar

84 Marries Cornelia, daughter of Cinna

80 Travels to Asia, where he becomes involved in scandal with Nicomedes, king of Bithynia, and wins Civic Crown at the Battle of Mytilene

73 Becomes member of the board of priests

69 Serves as *quaestor* (provincial administrator) in Further Spain

67 Marries Pompeia

65 Becomes *curule aedile* in charge of buildings and public order

63 Wins office of *pontifex maximus* (chief priest)

62 Elected *praetor* (state judge)

61 Becomes governor of Further Spain

60 Forms First Triumvirate with Pompey and Crassus

59 Serves as consul

58 Begins eight-year military campaign in Gaul; defeats the Helvetii and German tribes led by Ariovistus

called the Nervii

Veneti

of the Usipetes and the Tencteri; crosses

hes first expedition to Britain

Britain; daughter, Julia, dies

invading Parthian empire

d Gallic armies led by Vercingetorix at Alesia

River, igniting the Civil War

Greece; Caesar appointed dictator

Pharsalus

d in Egypt

andria; becomes involved with Cleopatra and

campaign against her political opponents

II in Asia Minor

nts of Pompeian army at Munda

where he is appointed dictator for life

e Senate house in Rome

Index

Roger Bruns is Director of Publications of the National Historical Publications and Records Commission in Washington, D.C. His books include *Knights of the Road: A Hobo History*, published by Methuen, Inc. He is also the author of *Thomas Jefferson* and *Abraham Lincoln* in the Chelsea House series WORLD LEADERS PAST & PRESENT.

Arthur M. Schlesinger, jr., taught history at Harvard for many years and is currently Albert Schweitzer Professor of the Humanities at City University of New York. He is the author of numerous highly praised works in American history and has twice been awarded the Pulitzer Prize. He served in the White House as special assistant to Presidents Kennedy and Johnson.